BEING IN LOVE

William Johnston, an Irish Jesuit, has spent much of his working life in Tokyo, where he still lives. He was formerly Professor of Religious Studies at Sophia University and Director of the Institute of Oriental Studies, both in Tokyo.

In 1989 he spent several months teaching at the University of Santa Clara in California, and then took a sabbatical year for teaching and study in his native Ireland.

William Johnston is the author of several books, including *The Inner Eye of Love*, *The Mirror Mind*, *The Wounded Stag* and his best-selling *Silent Music*. A fuller list is shown on the next page.

Books by the same author

available as Fount Paperbacks

The Inner Eye of Love
Letters to Contemplatives
Lord, Teach us to Pray

from other publishers

The Mysticism of "The Cloud of Unknowing"
The Still Point
Christian Zen

Translations

From the Japanese:
Silence by Shusaku Endo
The Bells of Nagasaki by Takashi Nagai

From the Middle English:
The Cloud of Unknowing and the
Book of Privy Counselling

Being in Love

———— ✳ ————

THE PRACTICE OF CHRISTIAN PRAYER

William Johnston

Fount
An Imprint of HarperCollinsPublishers

Fount Paperbacks is an Imprint of
HarperCollins*Religious*
Part of HarperCollins*Publishers*
77–85 Fulham Palace Road,
Hammersmith, London W6 8JB

First published in Great Britain
in 1988 by William Collins Sons & Co. Ltd
This edition first published in 1989
by Fount Paperbacks

5 7 9 10 8 6 4

A catalogue record for this book is
available from the British Library

ISBN 0 00 627476 5

Set in Sabon

Printed in Great Britain by
HarperCollinsManufacturing Glasgow

Religious experience at its roots is experience of an unconditional and unrestricted being in love. But what we are in love with remains something that we have to find out.

BERNARD LONERGAN

CONTENTS

ONE

Being in Love

You have asked me, Thomas, to write to you about the art of prayer; and in answer to your request I am putting down some ideas that may help both you and those whom you direct in your centre. I am indeed happy that you have decided to devote your life to personal meditation and to the guidance of others. This is a real calling, a vocation that puts you in the mainstream of modern life. For enlightened people everywhere are fast coming to the realization that what the modern world needs is prayer. Only prayer and the activity that springs from prayer can save our troubled generation from total destruction. Yes, prayer shakes the universe. It brings God's help. It leads to profound wisdom – a wisdom beside which the knowledge of scientist and scholar is but a tiny candle held up to the glorious light of the noonday sun. Persevere in the pursuit of this wisdom, prudently guide others in their inner journey, and you will find yourself on a path that leads not only to deep interior peace but also (wonder of wonders) to that world peace for which men and women everywhere so ardently long.

Though I have the temerity to write to you on this sublime subject, do not think of me as a highly enlightened master. I am just a poor fellow traveller stumbling along the way. Were I to speak more boldly I might say, with Paul, that I am an athlete running in the Isthmian games. I am not perfect nor have I arrived, but "I press on towards the goal for the prize of the upward call of God in Christ Jesus" (Philippians 3:12). So I make no big claims. I prefer to emphasize what you already know: that the real teacher of prayer is the indwelling Holy Spirit. Listen to his voice; follow his guidance, and you will go far on the path of mystical wisdom.

It may seem strange that I should write a treatise on prayer when we already have an abundance of such treatises. Don't we have *The Cloud of Unknowing*, *The Spiritual Exercises* of Ignatius, *The Interior Castle* of Teresa, and many other texts of great religious beauty? What more do we need?

Yes, Thomas, these are great classics. Read them again and again. Relish and savour their inspirational words. But remember, always remember, that they are (if you will permit me to use technical language) historically and culturally conditioned. That is to say, their authors were men and women of their time, speaking the language of their time, writing in the idiom of their time, breathing the atmosphere of their time. In short, they possessed the consciousness peculiar to their age. To understand them fully we must develop what scholars now call historical-mindedness: the facility to understand people in their historical context. Then we must penetrate to their trans-cultural message, translating it into the language and idiom of our day for the men and women of our day. What a challenge! For contemporary consciousness is very, very special.

It has become a truism to say that the human family is passing through a new stage in its turbulent march towards maturity, and that a new consciousness is coming to birth. Our way of thinking and feeling and reacting and relating has been shaped by a series of earthshaking social and cultural revolutions. For better or for worse we feel the influence of mighty prophets like Freud and Jung, Darwin and Einstein, Marx and Mao, Teilhard and Rahner, Gandhi and Merton. We have been changed by Hiroshima and Nagasaki and Chernobyl. We have seen men walking on the moon and travelling to the stars. We feel dread of nuclear war, fear of international terrorism, depression at pollution of the environment, panic at the prospects of a catastrophic epidemic of AIDS.

And a new religious consciousness is fast coming to birth. We witness in a new way the encounter of religions. Now Buddhists and Hindus, Jews and Muslims, Christians and agnostics live cheek by jowl, as mosques and synagogues, temples and churches mushroom in the big cities of the world. No one can escape the influence of other religions. Willy-nilly we are all drawn into an inner religious dialogue, with its shocks and challenges. Then there was the Second Vatican Council, with its opening to the world, its adaptation to modern thought, its compassion for the poor, its commitment to peace, and its passionate love for the Gospel. And there is the influence of Lourdes and Fatima and other great Marian shrines calling for radical conversion of mind and heart. All these factors have modified and changed that mysterious human entity which we now call consciousness. All these factors have shaped not only our way of thinking, of feeling, of reacting, of relating – they have also shaped our way of praying and of relating to God. How different is our mentality from that of the University of Paris where Ignatius studied! How different is our mentality from that of the pious girls who took the veil in sixteenth-century Avila!

One significant characteristic of the modern consciousness is its preoccupation with the inner world – what Bernard Lonergan calls "the shift to interiority". And with this comes a keen interest in meditation and mysticism. From Tokyo to Toledo and from Dublin to Delhi, men and women are practising zen or yoga or transcendental meditation or some form of mind-control. More and more enthusiasts flock to classes that teach relaxation or breathing or body-awareness or recitation of the mantra. Whereas previously meditation was the monopoly of religious people, we now find psychologists writing books, excellent books, on the art of meditation and on the higher consciousness to which meditation leads. Indeed, meditation is fast becoming an important element in therapy, with claims to heal chronic depression, to alleviate acute anxiety, to slow the ageing process. One constantly hears of people who through meditation have kicked ingrained habits of smoking or drinking or drug abuse. And, of course, meditation claims to enhance human potential, to stimulate creativity, to bolster self-confidence, to give inner peace.

And this poses a new question, a question that never entered the minds of our forebears: how can we distinguish between religious and secular meditation? What is it precisely that makes religious meditation be religious?

As you know, there are many definitions of religious experience. Let me here select one from a great Canadian theologian, Bernard Lonergan. "Religious experience", he writes, "at its roots is experience of an unconditional and unrestricted being in love. But what we are in love with remains something that we have to find out." This means that what makes religious meditation be religious (as opposed to the secular meditation practised for the development of human potential) is the dimension of love. This is a love that springs from the depths of the spirit, from the fine point or centre of the soul, from the core of the being where men and women are most truly themselves. It is not perfect love (for perfect love does not exist in our fallen world) but an ongoing, open-ended love that knows no limits. Just as the human mind has an infinite capacity for asking questions, so the human heart has an infinite capacity for love. Love can go on and on and on, "but what we are in love with remains something that we have to find out".

If one accepts this definition, some important conclusions follow.

The first is that religious experience is not something esoteric, not some strange appendix or addition to ordinary human experience. It is not just a luxury. It pertains to the very structure of human consciousness and to the process of being fully a woman or a man. Religious experience is an integral part of the human adventure. For what is more human than a boundless love that wells up from the inner depths, penetrating one's whole being and colouring all other loves?

The second important conclusion is that religious experience in its essence is not directly concerned with fidelity to law; it is not directly concerned with observance of rules and regulations; it is not explicitly concerned with commitment to formulas and doctrines and dogmas. Rather is it an inner movement or stirring which often lies dormant in the human heart until one fine day a person wakes up and asks: What is this that stirs in the depths of my being? And then he or she sets out on a quest that, although it may end with doctrines and laws, does not begin with them.

But now let me return to the so-called secular meditation. What about those who meditate in order to develop human potential, or to kick the habit of drugs, or to be liberated from chronic depression? Must we say that the religious dimension is lacking in their practice?

By no means! I know people who began meditation to develop human potential but continued because they felt

13

the call of unrestricted love. Or as they were liberated from
some addiction they began to experience a love without
conditions or limits. And the discovery of this love filled
them with such joy that the appeal of drugs or alcohol
paled into insignificance. Indeed, I myself had a little
meditation centre here in Tokyo. The core meditators were
Christians who knew they were loved by God and who
loved God in return. But others, agnostics or waverers,
joined us because they wanted inner peace. After a time
the self-styled agnostics (not all, but some) came to God;
and I believe that almost everyone felt flashes of the
unrestricted and unconditional love that I call religious
experience.

From this I conclude that while we can and must
distinguish theoretically between religious and secular
meditation, the practical work of discernment is much
more subtle. Face to face with people it is very, very
difficult, perhaps impossible, to say who enjoys religious
experience and who does not. And that brings me to a
practical point.

In your centre, Thomas, be open to receive agnostics or
atheists or anyone who shows interest. At first you need
ask no questions about their beliefs or unbeliefs or about
their life style. Simply teach them to sit and to breathe and
to attain to one-pointedness. God will come later. Indeed,
the day may come when these self-styled atheists reach the
pinnacle of mystical experience. But you must wait.

Throw your net wide. Welcome Buddhists and Hindus,
Jews and Muslims as brothers and sisters, and let them
meditate in their own way and in accordance with their
own beliefs. You know that there is now much talk, and
good talk, about solidarity with the poor. This is wonderful. But let us not forget another form of solidarity:
solidarity among those who pray. Perhaps it is part of
your vocation, Thomas, to work for such solidarity: to

direct a prayer centre that will open its welcoming doors to people of all religions and of no religion.

Two Ways?

MED.

With all this in mind let me suggest two ways of meditation that may be of value to you and those whom you guide.

The first centres on love. Take the biblical phrase: "God is love" (*1* John 4:8). Repeat it again and again in your heart. As you do so, savour it, relish it and you will find that it is sweet as honey in your mouth. "God is love . . . God is love . . . God is love." Repeat it at your own pace and rhythm. After some time you may wish to stop repeating it and to be silent, without words and without thought. This is a rich silence, a sacred silence, a precious silence, a mystical silence. This is indeed the threshold of mystical prayer. So treasure that silence lovingly until after some time (perhaps after one minute or perhaps after ten minutes) you get all distracted, and then you return to your biblical words: "God is love . . . God is love . . . God is love."

If you continue this loving practice for several weeks or months you may find that "God is love" keeps rising in your heart as you sit in the bus or stand on the train. It may fit into the rhythm of your body as you walk: your very footsteps and your breathing may be saying: "God is love . . . God is love . . . God is love." The refrain may continue even when you are busily engaged in some apparently absorbing occupation. It will be as though there were two levels in the mind. At one level you are absorbed in washing dishes or sweeping the floor or teaching mathematics or whatever; and at another level the refrain goes on: "God is love . . . God is love . . . God is love."

And then one day you may exclaim with a surge of ecstatic joy: "**God is love!** I never understood it before! For the first time in my life I know it is true; my whole being knows it and shouts out to the universe: **God is love**. Now my being is transformed and possesses the unshakeable conviction that God is love. How could anyone deny it? If only the world knew . . .! God is love . . . God is love . . . **God is love**."

But that is not the end. After a few months or years of repeating and savouring and relishing these words you may again cry out with sudden joy: "God is love! . . . I thought I understood it before, but I didn't. My former enlightenment was only the beginning. *Now* I know that God is love." And so you will go on and on and on, living this extraordinary message about the love of God. It can never be exhausted; you will never reach the end. For this is the mystery of mysteries, the mystery that lies at the heart of our Christian faith.

My second suggestion centres around the fact that prayer is a gift. Take the words of the disciples (you will find them at the beginning of Luke 11): "Lord, teach us to pray . . ." Or if you prefer, use the words: "Lord, teach me to pray." As before, repeat the words again and again. "Lord, teach me to pray . . . Lord, teach me to pray . . . Lord, teach me to pray." And be sure that the Lord will teach you to pray, for he has said: "Ask and it will be given you; seek and you will find; knock and it will be opened to you" (Matthew 7:7). It is as simple as that.

And yet in another way it is not so simple. Let me add a word from personal experience.

I myself used this prayer over a long period of time. In retrospect, however, I imagine that the Lord looked at me with a compassionate smile and said: "You ask for the gift of prayer? You know not what you ask. Can you drink of the chalice that I will drink?" For I thought naïvely that prayer was an ever sweet and tranquil gift bringing inner peace and joy and bliss. Now I know that while peace and consolation are assuredly there, the path leads inexorably to Gethsemane and to Golgotha. We cannot forget the agonized *Eloi, Eloi, lama sabacthani?*

But let not this deter you, Thomas. Remember that this path leads beyond Gethsemane and Golgotha to Galilee of the Resurrection. And as death comes many times in life, so also does resurrection. Indeed, you will find that joy wells up from the very place that formerly ached with pain. And so the joy of prayer far outweighs the suffering, as Paul well knew when he said that the sufferings of this time are not worthy to be compared with the glory that will be revealed to us. Yes, the glory is revealed to us even in this life, through enlightenments which are a foretaste of resurrection.

Persevere in this prayer, Thomas – if to it you feel called. Repeat the words; pause in the rich silence; and wait for the enlightenment that comes from the Spirit.

TWO

Prayer and the Body (1)

When I was a small boy I learned in my catechism that prayer is the raising of the mind and heart to God. This definition has its beauty and it has helped me, as it has helped millions of others, in the journey of life. Nevertheless I now see that it is (if you will permit me to return to the scholarly jargon) historically and culturally conditioned. It belongs to an age that idealized the mind and heart, while looking on the poor body as a troublesome and burdensome companion.

But that age, Thomas, has gone. We live in an age that is overawed by the enormous potential and mysterious energy that lies latent in the human body. Parapsychology, fast becoming a respectable science, reminds us of vibrations, auras, psychokinesis, alpha waves, energy fields, kirlian photography and all kinds of untapped psychic powers in our bodies. We are acutely aware of body language: that the eyes, the hands, the lips, the torso are sending out signals which a skilled person can quickly read. We know that certain neuroses are lodged in the very body and can be released and healed by kneading or massage or acupuncture. We are also aware of the wisdom of the body: if only we are attuned to our body, if only we are in touch with its inner dynamism, it will tell us when to eat and when to fast, what to eat and what not to eat, when to sleep and when to watch, when to exercise and when to rest. And if you say, "But tell me how to become attuned to my body!", the psychologist may answer with a single word: "Meditate!".

And one more important point. It is an old, old truth that fasting brings clarity of mind while over-eating causes drowsiness. But now we are acutely conscious of the role of **body chemistry** in our emotional and religious life. How body chemistry influences our mental and spiritual states! We know that certain chemicals (either preservatives in the food we eat or poisonous toxins in the air we breathe) can cause hyperactivity in children and acute anxiety in adults. We know that chemical addiction can drastically change the personality. We know that correct breathing brings tranquillity, and bad breathing can cause distress. We know that prolonged lack of sunlight can cause depression and mood disorder. We know that another Chernobyl could wreck not only the physical but also the psychological and emotional life of millions. And, of course, mesmerized by the scientific mentality, we attribute our depression, anger or anxiety to adrenalin or melatonin or hormones or some form of body chemistry.

And what a cult of health and longevity in our world! Think of the interest in diet and alternative medicine. And then the cult of exercise! From Osaka to Belfast, and from Beijing to Washington, men and women are running or swimming, skipping or skating, dancing or fencing. Paul told the Corinthians to emulate the athletes in the Greek games. Were he alive today he might point to the fresh young executives of Mitsubishi or General Motors. "They do it to receive a perishable wreathe but we an imperishable" (1 Corinthians 9:25).

And all this affects our approach to prayer. Any competent doctor or psychologist will smile if you say that religious experience is an activity of mind and heart alone. He or she knows that breathing and nerves and food and body chemistry are crucial elements in the religious adventure.

And so, Thomas, see meditation and prayer as holistic – as activities of the whole person. Raise to God not only your mind and heart but also your body and your breathing, your bones and your blood, your head and your hands and your feet. Keep back nothing from God. Your whole life belongs to him. Love God not with part of your being but with your whole being.

Yes, the great challenge of today is to pray with the body – to develop a praying body. Not that this is something new in the Judaeo-Christian tradition. Remember how Moses held up his hands in prayer while the Israelites fought their bloody battle in the valley below. "Aaron and Hur held up his hands, one on one side, and the other on the other side; so his hands were steady until the going down of the sun" (Exodus 17:12). That was body prayer with a vengeance. And the face of the same Moses was so transformed and transfigured through his converse with God that the Israelites could not bear to look at his radiant beauty. And then there was Miriam. Remember how she took a timbrel in her hand, and the women went out after her with timbrels and dancing, singing: "Sing to the Lord, for he has triumphed gloriously" (Exodus 15:16). And, of course, there was Elizabeth, who cried with a loud voice; and the gift of the Spirit penetrated every cell of her body so that the very babe leapt in her womb. The Israelites did not just raise their minds and hearts to God. Their bodies also were filled with the Spirit.

And the ideal of the praying body lived on, particularly in the monastic tradition, where it was axiomatic that one who wanted to pray must adopt a certain life style in which there were periods of fasting, a vegetarian diet, no alcohol, manual work in the fields, communal recitation of the scriptures, periods of rigorous silence. Interestingly enough, it was a life style strikingly similar to that adopted by Buddhist monks throughout Asia; and its ascetical principles spread to the active orders and even, in adapted form, to the whole Christian world.

But while this ascetical training had considerable value, it was marred by a certain contempt for the body that crept insidiously into the Christian consciousness. We find this already in New Testament times with the heresy of *docetism* which, rooted in a current notion that matter was evil, denied that Jesus had a real body. Something similar appeared in the various branches of *gnosticism* and, indeed, contempt for the body has kept raising its ugly head at various junctures throughout Christian history. Although the Christian community battled valiantly against this pernicious error – as is clear already in the first two epistles of Saint John – the dualistic idea that matter is evil continued to exert considerable influence on Christian life and thought; and continues to influence Christian life to this very day.

Then there was *Platonism* and *Neoplatonism*, which left their imprint on the mighty Augustine, standing like a giant at the source of Christian spirituality. For Plato the soul in the body was like a rider on a mettlesome horse. The rider must control and tame that horse; and in the same way the soul must tame and control the body. Obviously this way of thinking can lead to an abundance of chains, hair shirts, flagellations and the rest. Pious men and women even spoke of a holy hatred of the body, loudly proclaiming that greater is the one who conquers self than the one who conquers cities.

Here let me say in parenthesis that the same spectre of dualism has raised its ugly head in Hinduism and Buddhism. It is as though religious people everywhere are

21

tempted to cultivate the spirit at the expense of the body. One outstanding example is Mahatma Gandhi, whose love for peace and non-violence has captured the admiration of the civilized world. Even his most ardent admirers know that when it came to food and sex the Great Souled Mahatma was incorrigibly manichaean – one more example of a man of the spirit denigrating the body. But let me return to the Christian tradition.

The old asceticism held the field for many centuries and helped a lot of people. But it was unable to stand up to the medical and psychological discoveries of the twentieth century. People of the post-Freudian and post-Jungian era began to see that the training devised to develop a life of prayer was frequently leading to neurosis and psychological disturbance. And so a search began (and still continues) for an asceticism that would preserve the good things in the old, while integrating the valuable insights of the new. And we, Thomas – you and I – are part of that search.

One of the major defects of the old asceticism was its tendency to repress human instinct. We know now how disastrous such repression can be. If part of the psyche is repressed it will rebel: it may even act autonomously, causing bewildering problems. Repression of fear or anger or joy (yes, some people really are afraid to enjoy themselves) or sexuality or any basic instinct may result in anything from inner upheaval to acute and crushing depression. This latter is the worst. Get rid of depression, Thomas. The oldest Christian traditions say that sadness is from the devil.

In this area we are helped by modern psychology, for under its prudent guidance we are moving from a spirituality of control (the horse and the rider) to a spirituality of acceptance and integration. We are now encouraged to allow our emotions and feelings to rise to the surface of consciousness, when we recognize them, accept them, own them and integrate them. And all this enters into the process of prayer, particularly contemplative prayer.

Let me briefly make a few concrete suggestions to help you in this work of integration.

The first is **counselling**. As there is a time for everything under the sun, so there is a time for counselling. You will know intuitively when the time comes to look back on your life history, to allow fears and anxieties to surface, to reflect on your dreams, to expose your memory to the healing love of the Spirit – and to do this with a competent counsellor. Some people find this extremely liberating. It revolutionizes their prayer.

Parallel to this is **journal writing** – recording the main stages of your inner journey with non-judgemental sincerity. Of one of his famous characters Graham Greene writes that he never lied to his diary. And this advice I pass on to you, Thomas. Never lie to your journal, and never show it to anyone. Through its pages you will find that your unconscious becomes conscious, that your true self emerges, that you come to understand something about your life story, the mysterious inner journey on which you have embarked.

Rather than a journal, some people prefer to **sketch** with crayons **or** to **paint**. This, too, can be healing and liberating. We know that at one period in his life Jung drew his *mandala* (that symbol of wholeness) every day, and found it a powerful help in his journey towards individuation.

In general, Thomas, I advise you, as I would advise any contemplative, to develop your creative talents, whether they lie in the area of writing poetry or gardening or painting or calligraphy or photography or composing music or playing the guitar or whatever. The history of religion proclaims that contemplation is intensively creative – it has created superb works of art throughout Europe and Asia. So never stifle that creativity either in yourself or others. Let it flourish to the glory of God.

I have other concrete suggestions for the training of the body; but first let me pause to make an important aside.

I have said that body chemistry can profoundly affect the life of prayer. Let me now add a word of caution.

One of the pioneers in the field of drug culture was the brilliant Aldous Huxley, who did indeed have some religious insights. And Huxley, fascinated by certain cultures that used drugs to induce religious experience, asked the provocative question: If we can use organs and other musical instruments to create religious experience in our churches, why not use chemicals for the same purpose?

Ha! Ha! Don't take Huxley seriously on this point, Thomas. Don't experiment with drugs, and don't tolerate such experimentation at your centre. Organs and guitars may create the atmosphere in which you can love God with your whole heart and soul and mind and strength; but drugs will not do that. They may build up the very ego that should die. Besides, organ recitals will not damage your brain, make you a hopeless addict, or cause you to end your days in prison or in some institution. Perhaps Huxley's basic error was in identifying religious experience with higher consciousness and not with unrestricted love.

No, I do not advise drugs. What I do advise, however, is that you **train your body**, adopting a life style that is conducive to prayer. Pay attention to **diet**, remembering that what you eat and drink will affect your meditation. Experiment with fasting and find your way: for some people fasting is powerfully conducive to prayer, while for others it is disastrous. **Learn how to breathe**: you will find that as your breath becomes slow and rhythmical your body is permeated with a deep peace and quietude. **Learn body-awareness**, making use of some of the books that teach this art. I recommend *Sadhana* by Anthony de Mello. Together with this learn the necessary art of relaxation. All this will help you develop a praying body.

It is good to take up some **sport** like tennis or swimming or skipping or cycling. Running is now very popular and many people are discovering in it a meditative dimension. They find an inner unification stemming from the deep rhythmic breathing.

In this whole area you will learn a lot from the ancient tradition of **Asian asceticism**. From India to Japan, Asia has developed a culture of the body which, in my opinion, is superior to anything that has arisen in the West. This is a culture that leads to a *one-pointedness* which is of the greatest value in the life of prayer. You might like to take up yoga. At first the postures or *asanas* will be a preparation for prayer; but eventually you may find that they are not just preparation but real prayer in themselves. For yoga is body language and you will find in time that your body is talking to God: you won't need words. Or you may find that the *asanas* are penetrated with the silent presence of God. Similarly the breathing exercises or *pranayama* may at first be a way of cultivating inner stillness and harmony; but as time goes on you may discover *a prayer of the breath*. You may find that your breath is filled with the presence of God and that you are united with the Holy Spirit. About this I have written at some length in *The Mirror Mind* and need not repeat myself here.

You asked me about the value of **the lotus posture**. Yes, it is worth learning this perfect posture found all over Asia and even in ancient Egypt. It will help your contemplative life immensely, although I do not advise you to use this posture always. It is better to adapt your posture to your prayer. Different postures are good for different kinds of prayer.

Another Asian art of great value is the Chinese **Tai Chi**. Here again is a form of body language used throughout China. In Hong Kong I have watched men and women, old and young, practising this graceful art in the warm morning sun. Through it they learn breathing and rhythmic action; perhaps it, too, becomes a prayer-of-the-body.

Walking can be a wonderfully contemplative exercise. How many pilgrims have walked through Europe, India, China and Japan! I immediately think of the Zen monk and poet Basho, and of that charming pilgrim who walked through his native Russia reciting the Jesus prayer with his lips, with his heart and with his whole body. In walking one discovers one's inner rhythm, a rhythm into which a word or phrase can enter and repeat itself again and again and again.

In conclusion, let me suggest a practical exercise.

Go for a walk, Thomas, if possible in the countryside. Take the phrase, "God loves Thomas", and recite this phrase rhythmically as you walk. "God loves Thomas . . . God loves Thomas . . . God loves Thomas . . .". As you walk along, these words will enter into your very body. Soon you will discover that Thomas is no longer reciting the words: they are reciting themselves to the rhythm of your body: "God loves Thomas . . . God loves Thomas . . .". And you will come to the realization that God really does love Thomas, and that Thomas is blessed.

THREE

*

Prayer and the Body (2)

I have advised you, Thomas, to train your body for prayer, always remembering that there is an intimate connection between bodily health and spiritual vigour. I recall how, when once I was in deep spiritual crisis, a holy man said to me: "What you need is fresh air, exercise and good food. So take a vacation! Go to the hills or the sea! Walk!" That was good advice which I would gladly pass on to anyone in the throes of the dark night of the soul. Obviously I do not mean that fresh air, exercise and good food will solve all problems. I do mean, however, that the physical is one aspect of the complex phenomenon we call the dark night; and it is an aspect we must not neglect.

Yet life is full of paradox; and in this valley of tears there are broken bodies, lacerated bodies, mangled bodies, tortured bodies, crippled bodies, wasted bodies, starving bodies, bleeding bodies, dying bodies – and strangely enough these broken bodies often have more psychic energy than the bodies of the athletes. Indeed, they sometimes abound in that vital energy that Chinese medicine calls *chi*. This is the life force flowing through the meridians of the body, balancing *yin* and *yang*: it is an energy that frequently reaches a climax at the moment of death, when the face of the dying person is transfigured and becomes beautiful beyond all telling.

The praying body is frequently a sick body. Saint Teresa indicates that ordinarily one does not enter the seventh mansion (the apex of mystical prayer) without severe illness and pain. For me this is frightening, and I hope the great Carmelite is wrong. But it is certainly true that the weak bodies of the mystics were deeply prayerful, as was the crucified body of Jesus. Think of Paul weakened by shipwreck, beaten with rods, buffeted by a messenger of Satan. Think of the bleeding hands and feet of Francis of Assisi. Think of Takashi Nagai, and his deep mystical prayer as he lay dying of leukemia after the nuclear blast in Nagasaki. There are so many other examples. Only let me say that the people who come to your centre may be handicapped and sick or weak. Or there may be elderly people facing the physical diminishments that inexorably come with the ageing process, acutely aware that their being is being-unto-death. And surely these can have a praying body.

I take back nothing I have said about physical training for prayer. I take back nothing I have said about the value of health. Nevertheless I feel forced to think more deeply about the notion of the praying body. What, after all, does it mean to have a praying body?

Let me return to my starting point. "Religious experience at its roots is experience of an unconditioned and unrestricted being in love." Yes, and this love which we call religious experience pertains not just to the spirit but also to the body. The praying body is the loving body. It is the body permeated with the unrestricted, unconditional love that knows no limits. The praying body is the body that is filled with the Spirit of love: it possesses a beauty that the world cannot give. For the Christian it is the body that gives glory to Christ in accordance with the prayer of Paul that "Christ will be honoured in my body, whether by life or by death" (Philippians 1:20). And the same Paul writes to the Corinthians, "So glorify God in your body" (1

Corinthians 6:20). When we understand this we are in a position to face the disturbing Ignatian paradox that we strive might and main for health, but when sickness comes we welcome it as "no less a gift than health".

Now you may ask how one is to develop a loving body, and to this I have no simple answer. I only advise you to be open to the coming of grace. More concretely I advise you to be open to that earthshaking experience which I call **a conversion to the body**, about which let me say a further word.

Modern Christian spirituality speaks very much about the phenomenon of conversion. This is not conversion from one religion to another but an interior experience built on the gospel notion of *metanoia*, whereby one turns from sin and error to God, whereby one's heart of stone is replaced by a heart of flesh. Bernard Lonergan speaks of a threefold conversion: intellectual, ethical and religious; and other theologians speak of affective conversion as well as conversion to this, that or the other good thing. I want to speak of a bodily or physical conversion whereby one comes to love and accept one's body.

Such a conversion has many ramifications. I immediately think of Paul's assertion that husbands should love their wives as their own bodies: "For no man ever hates his own flesh but nourishes it and cherishes it as Christ does the Church" (Ephesians 5:29). Following Paul, when I speak of bodily conversion, I think of a turning in love not only to my own body but also to the community, to the whole material universe and to that mysterious entity which Paul calls the body of Christ.

And this conversion is a turning from sin. Here the sin stems from that strange and perverse human tendency (itself a consequence of original sin) to hate our bodies, to hate the material universe and even to hate the body of Christ. This tendency keeps cropping up at all times, in all places and in all religions, making it all the more difficult for humans to accept the baffling mystery of the incarnation: that the Son of God took a truly human body.

Now, Thomas, let me make an important statement. This conversion to the body – to the body of Christ – is the key to the Christian religion. I have already spoken of the heresy of *docetism* which refused to acknowledge that Jesus had a real body, and *docetism* was followed by a series of heresies which, rejecting the incarnation, refused to accept the body of Christ. That is to say, they refused to accept that the Word was God and that the Word became flesh and dwelt amongst us. And this was the error that included all other errors. Some of the church fathers held that the sin of the angels was precisely this: a refusal to accept the fact that God should become man.

Make no mistake about it, Thomas, that error is very much alive in the world today. It's all around us. It may be alive in you and me. Not that we deny the incarnation or the divinity of Jesus with our lips, but that our acceptance is not total and complete. We need enlightenment, realization, conversion. More and more we need, through meditation, to let this great mystery penetrate our minds and hearts and bodies: that the Word was made flesh and dwelt amongst us and that Jesus is Lord. Just as the early Christian community, while fighting against errors outside, had to purify itself from its heresy inside; so we must grow in understanding of this awe-inspiring mystery, which gives the lie to every theory that matter is evil.

It is interesting to note that in stressing the reality of the incarnation the Christian community of the fifth century turned to the Virgin Mary. The Councils of Ephesus and

Chalcedon stressed that she was *theotokos* or mother of God, and not just *Christo-tokos* or mother of Christ, as the monk Nestorius had claimed. In this way they avoided dividing Jesus into two parts, one human and the other divine; and they maintained the purity of the scriptural teaching that the Word became flesh. And Mary's title of Mother of God is as theologically important today as it was in the fifth century.

And so the conversion of the Christian community to the body of Christ goes on. Never is it completed. Never will it be completed until he comes in glory. The Second Vatican Council was indeed a conversion to the material world – to the world of art and poetry and science, to the afflicted bodies of the poor and the sick, to the whole world of matter. My guess is that the next General Council (whether it be Vatican III or Manila I or whatever) will treat mainly of the person of Jesus Christ. It will be an ongoing conversion of the Christian people to the historical Jesus of Nazareth, who died for our sins and rose from the dead.

As you know, it is not my intention here to write a treatise on speculative theology. I am thinking principally of your life of prayer and of your meditation centre. So let me draw some practical conclusions.

The first is: let your prayer be incarnational. We Christians are not called to a prayer of pure spirit that would reject either our own body or the body of Jesus. No, no, we are called to a prayer that is fully human. (Sometimes people speak of a prayer that transcends the human condition, but I cannot see such prayer as being Christian.) Needless to say, this prayer includes mystical contemplation, than which nothing could be more human. Alas, there is a popular misconception that mystical prayer is a prayer of pure spirit. Nothing could be further from the truth. The mystical silence, the emptiness, the darkness and the void are, and must be, profoundly incarnational. But about this I shall speak later.

That the prayer in your centre may be truly incarnational, I advise you to give pride of place to **the two tables**: the table of the word and the table of the eucharist.

By **the table of the word** I mean the reading of the scriptures. All of your prayer should ultimately be based on Sacred Scripture. Not that you must always hold the words of scripture in your conscious mind – it may be that your prayer is in empty silence – but that they should be the ultimate source of your religious experience. If your silence is to be authentic the word must be living in your unconscious, living in the subliminal areas of your mind, giving birth to the mystical silence. And so I urge you to read the scriptures again and again, and to recite them in common so that your deepest mind may be a storehouse of archetypal images from the Bible.

The second table is the eucharist. Give to the eucharist a place of honour in your centre. I mean not only the celebration but also the subsequent reservation of the sacrament which proclaims the presence of Jesus, human and divine. Here you will honour not only the spirit of Jesus but also his body. Jesus himself will be living in you, and you will cry out with Paul: "I live, now not I but Christ lives in me." Moreover, through the eucharist Jesus will live in your community, uniting you and making you realize that through the one bread you are one body.

To these tables I add a third: **the table of life**. Let your life flow into your prayer. Let your life nourish your prayer. Remember how Mary prayed by pondering in her heart the events that surrounded her journey to Bethlehem: "Mary kept all these things pondering them in her heart" (Luke 2:19). And in the same way you can ponder in your heart all that is happening in your life and in the world, particularly the suffering world. This will nourish your prayer and keep your feet on the ground.

If you honour these three tables, some important consequences will follow.

The first is that you will build a community of love. You will discover the simple but profound truth that Christian prayer leads to deep human love. This is a theme that occurs again and again in the writings of the great Teresa. She speaks about raptures and visions and voices, but her main thesis, to which she always returns, is: "Love your neighbour. You cannot really know whether you love God; but you can have some idea whether or not you love your neighbour." And this, of course, is both scriptural and eucharistic.

And so in your prayer centre let loving community develop. By this will everyone know that you pray, if you love one another. Be sure, moreover, that your centre of prayer is also a centre of concern, of loving concern for the poor, the sick, the afflicted, the tortured, the downtrodden – concern for the body of Christ suffering throughout the world. Be aware of the crises of our world: the arms race, the nuclear threat, the pollution of the atmosphere, international terrorism, the scourge of AIDS. Such concern will follow automatically from meditation that takes its nourishment from the table of the word and the table of the eucharist.

Then be sure that a place of honour is given to the Mother of God. She will lead you to the three tables and to love for the suffering world.

I still stand by the holy man who told me to take exercise, fresh air and good food, though now I see a deeper meaning in his counsel. He was not – as I then thought –

telling me to make concessions to weak human nature. By no means. He was urging me in a practical way to love my body, to love the material universe and to love the body of Christ.

Let me conclude this chapter with a practical exercise that may lead to bodily conversion.

Sit before the tabernacle. Be present to the Risen Jesus who is before you. His body is there as well as his blood, his soul, his divinity. Just be present without words. Now make a spiritual communion by which, through your longing and desire, you receive him into your body. "He who eats my flesh and drinks my blood dwells in me and I in him" (John 6:56). This is the the true bread that came down from heaven and gives life to the world. Be silent for some time. Perhaps you need no words at all. After a while recite with relish the words of Paul: "It is no longer I who live but Christ who lives in me" (Galatians 2:20). Or, if you wish, repeat again and again the words of that well-known prayer:

> Soul of Christ, sanctify me.
>
> Body of Christ, save me.
>
> Blood of Christ, inebriate me.

Be silent, inebriated by the body and blood of Christ. And know that your mind and body are being transformed.

FOUR

*

Ways of Praying

There are many ways of praying, as there are many ways
of expressing love. If people ask me how they should pray
I throw the ball back with the question: "How do you like
to pray? How do you pray when you are at your best?
Your way is the best way – for you."

Some people are drawn spontaneously to prayer. From
childhood they have enjoyed intimacy with God. They like
to talk to God, to bring before him their problems, their
joys, their sorrows, their anxieties. If they have to make a
big decision they bring it to him, asking for his counsel. Or
they complain to God (as did Job and many biblical figures)
asking why he has treated them so badly. God is their
friend, their best friend and, in a sense, their only friend,
as he was the friend of Moses. I am reminded of Thomas
More who refused to take the oath of allegiance to bluff
King Hal. "Aren't you the king's good friend?" they asked.
"Ay", he replied. "The king's good friend; but God's friend
first."

God's friend first! People who talk to God as their
intimate friend, Thomas, are nature's mystics. Leave them
to their friendship with God. Don't force them into any
other method. God himself will teach them, and the
friendship will develop through words to silence (is not
silence part of every true friendship?) and on to words
again. It may develop in a way you and I do not understand. Nor need we understand.

It sometimes happens that people have a favourite phrase or word (shall I call it a mantra?) to which they constantly return. Amongst Christians the name of Jesus is very popular. I find that lots of Christians are drawn spontaneously to repeat the word "Jesus". And sometimes they recite the name unceasingly: not only during formal prayer but all during the day. Standing on the bus or sitting in the train the name keeps rising up in their minds and hearts and bodies. They may recite just the word Jesus; or they may use the famous formula: "Lord Jesus, Son of God, have mercy on me a sinner!" Or they may use some other form of this powerful prayer: "Jesus, I love you", "Jesus, in you I trust". The whole Christian tradition proclaims that the name of Jesus has power to shake the universe.

Or it may be that their favourite phrase is: "Come, Holy Spirit!" This prayer is popular with active people who must constantly make decisions. They believe that the Spirit gives them light and wisdom in the small and great decisions of daily life.

Or again some people constantly pray to Mary, the Mother of God: "Holy Mary, pray for us." As they make this prayer they pass the beads through their fingers, and in this way they are praying not only with their hearts but also with their fingers. So Mary is ever with them, protecting and guiding and loving.

Again it sometimes happens that people have their own peculiar word. This word has not been given them from outside but has arisen spontaneously in their hearts; and for them it is very precious. This word may be "God" or "Love" or "Peace" or "Joy". Usually it is a short word; for a short word, said the old authors, pierces heaven. Again, their whole life centres around this word which keeps resounding within, even in the midst of a busy life.

Or it may be a sound. Here, however, let me say that we Christians must do more study on prayer through sound. The repetition of a sound (even when it has no explicit meaning) can bring us to subtle states of consciousness where we encounter God. A good example of this is the church bell or the bell in your meditation hall. I am reminded of the great Takashi Nagai of Nagasaki who, while still an agnostic, was drawn to God by the bells of the angelus. And the bells of Nagasaki continued to ring in his heart, reminding him to offer his life for peace in the world.

Closely allied to this is the inner singing of one's favourite hymn. Yes, some people like to sing interiorly: to sing in their hearts a hymn or song or canticle which may lead them to inner silence and deep contemplation. The song takes care of the noises and snakes at the more superficial layers of the psyche, thus allowing them to plunge down to the centre of the soul. Or again there is praying or singing in tongues – the *glossolalia* that well up from the inner depths. I know people who, alone in the mountains or driving a car, sing out in tongues to the glory of God.

And one more point. You need not make a clear distinction between mental and vocal power. Some people have their favourite vocal prayer that they recite again and again. It may be the *Memorare*, that bold prayer of Bernard of Clairvaux. *Never* was it known that *anyone* who turned to Mary was forsaken. Saint Ignatius suggests that we take each word of a vocal prayer and turn it over in our minds and hearts with love and relish.

Again, some people may be drawn to the prayer of petition. They are constantly praying to God for themselves or for their friends or for the world, knowing that intercessory prayer is central to the Bible and to the life of Jesus. Remember how Jesus said to Simon: "I have prayed for you" (Luke 22:32). I have asked myself, when did Jesus pray for Simon? Did the thought of his friend Simon Peter rise into his mind during those nights of prayer on the mountain? And then there is Paul. Read the introduction to each of his epistles and you will find a Paul constantly praying for his people – that they may be endowed with true wisdom, and that Christ may dwell in their hearts through faith. "I remember you in my prayers" keeps echoing though his incisive sentences.

But regarding the prayer of petition let me add a word of caution. The old authors used to say shrewdly that we can be more attached to God's gifts than to God. Be careful about that, Thomas. You may humbly ask; but you cannot manipulate God. You cannot pressurize God into giving you things. Remember those men who came early to the vineyard and then demanded more money than their contract had stipulated. But the Master said: "Am I not free? Don't try to manipulate me." So having made your request leave everything to him. If you do this you will find that he answers with a generosity beyond your wildest dreams. If instead of "Give us wine" you say with Mary, "They have no wine", you will find that he turns the water into wine – the best wine, that goes down smoothly, gliding over lips and teeth.

Some people's whole prayer is "Thanks be to God!" During their busy day they constantly thank God for the wind and the rain, for the people they meet and the people they don't meet, for the ups and downs, for the successes and the failures, for the frustrations and the joys. I once heard a Japanese monk say: "Unless you can say *Deo Gratias* every moment of your life, you have not arrived at enlightenment."

But again let me add a word of caution. Be emotionally honest! Don't say "Thanks be to God" unless you really mean it. If you feel angry with God it is much better to tell him so than to utter an insincere *Deo Gratias*. Remember how the psalmist talks turkey to God. Don't be afraid to express your true feelings!

Again, some people like to pray with the breath. They may recite the Jesus prayer or some other phrase to the rhythm of their breathing, or they may simply be aware of their breath without words. During the day they sometimes pause to breathe consciously and to become aware of the breath coming in and going out. About this way of the breath I have written in some detail in *The Mirror Mind*.

Then there is the so-called application of the senses. In this prayer you take a scene from the gospels and imagine that you are really present, seeing, hearing, talking to the characters and taking part in the living drama. In his meditation on hell (which, needless to say, is a bit controversial in our modern world) Ignatius tells the retreatmaker not only to see and hear but also to smell and to touch. In this way he is leading to an experience of those mysterious interior senses, described vividly by Teresa of Avila, whereby one sees but not with the bodily eyes, hears but not with the bodily ears, smells but not with the bodily nose, touches but not with the bodily hands. And yet it is a prayer of the body – for those interior senses are not pure spirit but very refined bodily feelings, whose secret wealth psychology has not yet mined.

A variation of this application of the senses is to imagine that Jesus walks into your room and says that he loves you, and asks for your love. Hear his words. Hear him call you by name. Imagine him at your side. This is not just make-believe. For the Risen Jesus is walking with you through life, as he walked with the two disciples on the road to Emmaus.

*

I have spoken about savouring and relishing the scriptures, but there is also a way of wrestling with the scriptures as Jacob wrestled with the angel. I think of the Zen koan where the meditator is faced with a baffling problem with which he struggles until he can *identify* with it and make it his own. In the same way you can take some of the shocking paradoxes of the Gospel and turn them over and over until the inner meaning reveals itself not to your intellect but to your life. Take, for example, "Blessed are the poor". This is a shocking paradox (for most of us deep down believe that blessed are the rich), but we have heard it so often that it has lost its power to jolt. Repeat this phrase; wrestle with it; live it. Only when you *become poor* (and that is what I mean by identification) will you realize with great joy the profound meaning. And so for the other beatitudes. They are all shockers if only we can read them as if for the first time. And this kind of meditation brings about a conversion, a revolution of consciousness, a joyful enlightenment.

I recommend this kind of meditation with the parables of the Gospel. Take a parable and read it aloud. Then read it again. Then again. And again and again. Read it before you go to sleep at night. This is important: for your unconscious is working in a very special way during the night. Then read it when you waken in the morning. In this way you may find some day that your consciousness has been revolutionized by a wonderful insight into the word of God.

Or there is the practice of copying the scriptures. I learned this art from Buddhists who love to copy their sutras. It is an exercise in calligraphy, but it matters not that one's Chinese characters be beautiful. What matters is that through copying one acquires the mind or consciousness of the Buddha. And in the same way one can copy the gospels, thus acquiring the mind or consciousness of

Christ. This is done by many Christians in Japan, and I myself love to do it.

To Catholics, Thomas, I always recommend prayer before the tabernacle. Here they can express that intimate friendship with Jesus about which I have spoken. Here they can speak to the Lord about what is in their mind and heart. Here they can be silent in the depths of contemplation. Throughout the Catholic world, in the churches of Manila or New York or London, you always find people kneeling or sitting before the tabernacle, petitioning or thanking or praising God. Encourage such prayer in your centre and, as far as possible, keep your chapel open to the people.

I have suggested many ways of praying, and perhaps you have noted that sooner or later they all lead to that silence wherein you rest in the presence of God. The old theologians expressed this by saying that all forms of prayer converge finally on contemplative prayer. No matter where you begin, you end with contemplation.

And so whenever you enter into this loving silence and deep peace, stay there. Remain in the silence until (as may well happen) you get overwhelmed with distractions: then return to the repetition of your word or phrase until it once more leads you into the silence. In contemplative prayer there is an interplay of words and silence. As time goes on you will find that words rise out of the silence, and silence rises out of the words.

Silence is valuable. But do not make a fetish of silence, and do not make a fetish of words. What matters is neither silence nor words but faith and love. You remember how, in the Sermon on the Mount, Jesus told us not to prattle along with many words, like the Gentiles. And he might equally well have said: "Do not use a lot of silence like the

Gentiles . . ." For, as I have said, what matters is faith and love. "Religious experience at its root is experience of an unconditioned and unrestricted being in love."

And this brings me to another important point. You may have heard it said that in prayer any word or phrase will do: "It doesn't matter what phrase you use, since the repetition of any sound will lead you to an altered state of consciousness or an enhanced state of awareness." This way of thinking, Thomas, is a snare. For the fact is that in Christian prayer the all-important dimension is (if I may return to my starting point) unrestricted and unconditional love. When you recite the name or any religious word your being will be filled with love for the God whom you invoke. But if you keep rattling on with some word or phrase or sound as the Gentiles do, without faith and love – of what value is this? Even if it does lead you to an altered state – so what? Never forget that what matters is love.

In some religious traditions, it is true, you are told to be "hypnotized" by the sound. But in the Christian life, it is much better to be lovingly hypnotized by Jesus to whom the word points. Once hypnotized by him it does not matter what word or sound you use. What matters is that you be filled with the Spirit. Sometimes, as Paul says, the Spirit will pray within you with sighs too deep for words; and at other times the same Spirit will cry out: "Abba, Father!"

From what I have said, Thomas, it will be clear that there are endless ways of praying: the way of the name, the way of the breath, the way of the mantra, the way of petition, the way of thanksgiving, the way of silence, the way of presence, the way of savouring the scriptures, the way of wrestling with the scriptures, the way of intimate friendship with God, and countless other ways. Needless to say, these ways overlap in such wise that, for example, people who follow the way of the name may at the same time follow the way of the breath. Or at one time in their lives they will follow the way of petition, and at another time they will follow the way of thanksgiving.

It is important that you find your way and help others to do so. But (and this is important) never think that you have found your definitive and final way. Never, for example, say: "This is my way and I will follow it until I die"; or, "This is my mantra and I will never change". No, no. Prayer is a process or a journey. As you advance you outgrow earlier ways of praying; and methods that once helped will (if you cling to them) become a hindrance. Indeed you will outgrow all methods and come to resonate with the words of Saint John of the Cross that the way is no way. By this he means that we cannot cling to any path or methodology or way; we cannot cling to plans and maps. God calls the shots and we follow after.

Life is full of surprises, they say; and no life has more surprises than the life of prayer.

FIVE

※

Grades of Prayer

When I was a student I had to study a subject called
ascetical and mystical theology, which treated of every
aspect of the so-called spiritual life and in particular of the
grades of prayer. From the earliest times Christian spiritual
writers had divided and classified the life of prayer into
such stages as the purgative way, the illuminative way and
the unitive way. Or they spoke symbolically of prayer as a
ladder – a ladder of perfection. Or they described it as a
journey: either a journey up the mountain, or a journey to
the inner depths of one's being. Later theologians began to
draw maps of prayer, using less symbolical language.

This Christian heritage is rich indeed and merits profound study. Here, however, I must content myself with a
brief outline of the grades of prayer as described by the
mystical theologians of the last two centuries.

The first stage in the spiritual journey was that of
discursive prayer. This was the prayer of the three powers
of the soul: the memory, the understanding and the will.
One was told to *remember* or recall some passage from the
scriptures (special emphasis was given to passages about
the passion and death of Jesus) or some basic Christian
truth such as the four last things. Having remembered, one
then tried to *understand* the mystery. Then with the *will*
one was encouraged to make a colloquy or prayer to God
expressing one's love or gratitude or trust or whatever
sentiment suggested itself. And finally one was encouraged

to make a practical resolution to live out this truth in one's daily life.

In this prayer the understanding was important because through it one attained to conviction about the basic truths of one's faith. But most important of all was the will, since it put one directly in contact with God. That God cannot be known by the discursive intellect but that he can be loved with the will was an old and venerable saying. And so the memory and understanding was preparatory to the activity of the will which loved God, spoke to God and made resolutions to serve God.

Discursive prayer was the way of beginners. It was followed by a second stage called **affective prayer** which was the way of proficients. Now the spade work had been done, reasoning and thinking were over, and one made aspirations or ejaculations of love or trust or whatever one felt called to. This was a prayer of refined feeling sometimes accompanied by tears or spontaneous outcries to God. Unlike discursive meditation, which was hard work, this affective prayer was considered effortless and liberated.

Next came **the prayer of simplicity**, a term first used by the great French preacher Jacques Bossuet. Very similar to affective prayer this consisted in the repetition of one single word or phrase or ejaculation. One repeated the word again and again as I have described in the last chapter – it was a simplified form of affective prayer. It is recorded that Saint Francis Xavier spent a whole night repeating the words, "My God and my All". This prayer was also called "acquired contemplation" and (when it contained periods of wordless silence) "the prayer of simple regard".

All the above forms of prayer were considered ordinary, meaning they they could be attained by human effort assisted by ordinary grace. The next step, however, was something of a leap into what was called **infused contemplation** or extraordinary prayer. This was characterized by an experiential sense of God's presence. We all know by faith that God is omnipresent; but infused contemplation was the positive experience of this presence. "I know that God is present within me or around me; I experience it; I cannot doubt it" is the claim of such a contemplative. But she has no clear-cut concept of her God. She feels that she is in a cloud of unknowing, with only an obscure sense of presence.

Again, the contemplative may say: "I could not cause this experience myself. It is something given; it is pure gift." And this claim made theologians speak of the direct action of God.

Note, however, that in the Christian tradition not everyone was encouraged to enter into the way of infused contemplation. For this was a privileged way; and one must wait at the gate of the sheepfold until the Good Shepherd invited one to enter. Mystical writers spoke of certain signs by which a person might know that the time to enter had indeed come. About these signs I have written in some detail in *Silent Music*, and it is sufficient here to refer you to that book.

Within infused contemplation there were many stages or grades. Whereas the earlier stages of prayer were described in scholastic terms taken from Greek philosophy, the theologians turned principally to Teresa of Avila for the more advanced stages of mysticism. The great Spanish Carmelite was not a trained theologian (though she is now a doctor of the Church) but her symbol of an interior castle in the centre of which dwells God – this symbol was (and still is) of the greatest value in describing the mystical descent. Guided by Teresa the theologians spoke of the prayer of quiet, the prayer of union, the prayer of transforming union. They also turned to another Spanish Carmelite, Saint John of the Cross, and spoke in terms of dark nights. About the more advanced stages of prayer I will speak later. Here let me make a few comments on the earlier stages of the path.

Today, Thomas, there is a reaction against discursive prayer. People call it a head trip; they say it contains too much theologizing; they say we must get out of the head and into the heart or the senses; they quote Teresa to the effect that prayer consists not in much thinking but in much loving. They say that conceptualization is a hindrance to contemplative prayer.

I can understand these criticisms. I know that in my time we got an overdose of discursive prayer. In some places it was considered the only safe way of prayer, and novices were forced into a discursive straitjacket from which they could not escape. Moreover this discursive prayer was called Ignatian – a misnomer because Ignatius taught many different kinds of prayer.

Yet, having said all this, let me assure you that it is a good, solid form of prayer. If people like to pray this way, don't discourage them. Only let them be open to grow into the realms of affective prayer and the prayer of simplicity. Many people have begun with discursive prayer and ended up as consummate mystics.

Indeed, the path traced out by those mystical theologians – discursive to affective to simple prayer to infused contemplation – is very valuable provided we do not consider it a road everyone must necessarily travel. I myself have some reservations – not about the ways of praying but about the terminology that was used.

Acquired and *infused* are not good terms. All prayer is infused; all prayer is a gift. Without the Holy Spirit we cannot say, "Jesus is Lord" nor can we say, "Our Father". The old authors knew this, of course, and they spoke of ordinary grace and special grace. Nevertheless this terminology is not satisfactory (since all grace is special), and instead of infused contemplation I prefer to speak of mystical contemplation.

Again the terminology *ordinary* and *extraordinary* is not good. Mystical contemplation is not extraordinary, it is very ordinary. All Christians, I believe, are called to it; and when they follow this path they become their true selves, their very ordinary selves. They become plain John or Jane, plain Kate or Ken.

Again, we should be slow to speak of the *direct action of God*. Our increased knowledge of the unconscious, and our modern distinction between the ego and the self let us see that there can be movements in the psyche that are beyond our control. Such movements may look like the direct action of God when in fact they are movements of the unconscious and less known parts of our own psyche.

I said that in modern times there is a reaction against discursive prayer. This, Thomas, is not completely new. There has always been tension between the advocates of mysticism and the advocates of dialectic. The teachers of mystical contemplation rightly emphasize that it is disastrous to cling to discursive meditation when the time for quiet and wordless silence has come. Thinking and reasoning, they insist, will only smother the tiny contemplative flame; thinking and reasoning will crush something beautiful that is coming to birth in the depth of the soul. Saint John of the Cross flares up in anger at spiritual directors who force contemplatives to think discursively. Such directors, he says, are like blacksmiths pounding and hammering when they should stand back and allow the tiny seed to grow. So never act like a blacksmith, Thomas. Let the delicate flower develop and bloom in the hearts of people called to the deeper mansions.

At the same time beware of exaggeration. There was current in medieval spirituality a saying of the French mystic Richard of St Victor that "when contemplation is born reason dies". Richard wrote fancifully that just as Rachel died in giving birth to Benjamin so reason dies in giving birth to contemplation. And he warned would-be contemplatives and their directors not to strangle their children at birth; that is to say, not to murder the beautiful child called contemplation.

Taken as practical advice this literary use of the scriptures is wise and valuable. It is a powerful way of telling us to stop reasoning when the time has come for silent contemplation. But never forget that it is pious hyperbole. For when contemplation is born reason does not die. *Reason is purified*. It would be strange indeed if the gift of contemplation were to annihilate something so humanly beautiful as reason. The fact is that the contemplative must stop reasoning, must bury thinking beneath a cloud of forgetting – but only for a time. When the work of purification is completed, the contemplative reasons again. When the cloud of forgetting has done its work, the contemplative remembers again.

Yes, reasoning and thinking are an important part of human life which must never be abandoned. Just as we must use both sides of the brain, so we must use both intuitive and rational faculties if we wish to lead a balanced life. I have no hesitation in saying that some use of the three powers of the soul is essential in a life devoted to prayer. If your prayer is quiet and contemplative without reasoning and thinking, then *outside the time of prayer* you must use your intellectual powers. Concretely, outside the time of prayer you must study the scriptures, read the commentators, study theology. You must keep yourself informed about the suffering of the world: the problems of hunger, oppression, torture, persecution, nuclear war, the arms race, pollution of the environment. Without this your contemplation will make you one-sided and may even withdraw you from life.

Contemplation leads one into silence; but it frequently happens that, as time goes on, the reasoning powers become active again. From the very core of the inner experience words rise up. And if this happens to you, Thomas, let the words come. Don't suppress them. Don't chase them away. Don't bury them beneath a cloud of forgetting. For these are contemplative words and this is the contemplative reasoning that arises in a purified mind.

I myself believe that the tremendous intellectual output of Thomas Aquinas was a direct consequence of his mystical contemplation. The *Summa Theologica* was not only the result of much reading and study, it was a verbal expression of his mystical experience. The same holds true for Augustine and the other theological geniuses who were mystics. Contemplation never killed their reason: it purified it.

So make it your aim to balance reasoning and contemplation in your life. Only remember that the wisdom found in prayer far excels any knowledge found through dialectic. The knowledge of the scholar beside the wisdom of the mystic is like a candle beside the noonday sun.

SIX

*

Prayer in Nature

Let me now, Thomas, suggest to you a way of prayer that is deeply rooted in the Christian tradition and continues to make an immense appeal to the men and women of our day: prayer in the world of nature. The Gospel tells us that Jesus prayed in the mountains and in the wilderness. His parables speak about the fields and the seed and the sower – about the great mystery of life and growth. They reveal a Jesus profoundly familiar with the world of agriculture.

And Christian monasticism, following Jesus, has always seen a close relationship between manual work in the fields and contemplative prayer in one's cell. It is as though contact with the soil and silent labour with the crops draws the monk into religious experience, uniting him with the living God. And let me here add that Buddhist monasticism has the same insight. For one who would walk the path to enlightenment, manual work is as important as silent sitting in the lotus posture.

And then there is the practice of communing with nature. As a small boy in Liverpool I had to read William Words-worth, whose poetry speaks of an invisible presence run-ning through the streams and valleys and mountains and flowers. The daffodils "flash upon that inward eye which is the bliss of solitude". Some scholars said that Words-worth was a pantheist; but even as a kid I questioned that.

Somehow I knew that Wordsworth was speaking of a fairly common religious experience: that of communing with God present in the mountains and the ocean. One can pause for a moment and experience or feel a presence, immanent or transcendent, beyond all that meets the eye or strikes the ear. Surely this is closer to nature mysticism than to pantheism.

So be open, Thomas, to this mysterious and obscure sense of presence. God is there: in the mountains and the ocean, in the flowers and the birds, in the trees and the fields. Walk through the green fields or the brown bog; or walk beside the ocean, listening to every sound, aware of the beauty and, above all, conscious of the enveloping presence that hovers over everything. This can be exhilarating prayer. For God is wonderfully present in all things, working in all things, giving himself to us in all things. We cannot see him or touch him; but we can sometimes sense his presence: his healing presence. When your mind and heart are troubled, walk and look at nature. Feel the air and the rain washing your body and cleansing your spirit. Eat and drink copiously from the energizing, liberating, healing, life-giving table of life.

Learn from those poets and mystics who talk to the mountains and the sea, opening their minds and hearts to the response. Such is the language of the psalmist and of Isaiah. Such is the way of Francis of Assisi, who preached to the birds. Such is the way of Saint John of the Cross, who begged the woods and thickets to tell him the whereabouts of his beloved. Such is the way of many simple (and not so simple) people who talk to their plants. And then there is that happy Shakespearian character (wasn't it the exiled Duke in the Forest of Arden?) who found tongues in trees, books in the running brook, sermons in stones and good in everything. How much living theology is written in the book of nature!

Read again and again the sixth chapter of Matthew, which speaks of the lilies of the field and the birds of the air. Jesus tells us to *look*. So take his words literally. Look at the birds of the air. Look at the lilies of the field. Relish their beauty – not even Solomon in all his glory was arrayed as one of these. As you walk along that path in the countryside or climb the road that winds up the mountain, look at the grass and the birds; stop for a while to look at that cow or that sheep or that horse. Look at them! Some good people have never looked at anything in their whole lives, because while they are looking at one thing they are thinking of another – or are making plans for the future.

And while you look and listen, keep in mind the Gospel message to let go of your anxieties. How we love our anxieties! How we cling to them! How we wallow in them! But the Gospel says: Let them go! Do not be anxious. Away with worries and nagging preoccupations. Your Father knows what you need. So do not be anxious. Your Father loves you. So do not be anxious. If you ask for a fish he will not give you a serpent. So do not be anxious. Only one thing is necessary, as Mary discovered when she sat lovingly at the feet of Jesus.

And now go one step further. Get rid not only of anxieties but of all thought – of reasoning and thinking and conceptualizing and planning for the future. As you look at nature don't *think about* the lilies and the birds. Don't put names to the various species of plants. Don't get involved in botany or ornithology! Look and listen and learn to be – like the flowers of the field and the birds of the air.

What a wonderful teacher is Mother Nature! She teaches us to be. And that is the lesson we need. We are so much given to frenetic activity, to workaholism, to getting things done, to glorying in achievement. We live in a society that gives Nobel Prizes and other prizes for achievement; but are there any prizes for those who have mastered the art of being? We need to recall the old Thomistic paradox that being is active, being is creative, being achieves very, very much. And *what you are* is more important that *what you do*.

And this lesson is particularly revelant for the sick, the imprisoned, the aged – for those reduced to inactivity who feel their lives are useless because they are no longer productive. Let such people know that by being they construct a field of energy; by being they bear fruit like the vine; by being they give glory to God. Let them know that they are called to the highest wisdom and that they may be the real architects of world peace.

And let me in this context suggest one more way of prayer: contemplation or awareness of your own body. Take those other words from the same chapter of Matthew: "Is not life more than food and the body more than clothing?" Again, don't *think about* your life and your body; *experience* them. And you can do this through your breathing: not by controlling your breath but by being aware of it. If it is short, it is short; if it is long, it is long. Recall that famous Buddhist text: "When you draw in a deep breath, O Monks, be aware you are drawing in a deep breath. When you draw in a shallow breath, O Monks, be aware you are drawing in a shallow breath. When you draw in a medium-sized breath, O Monks, be aware that you are drawing in a medium-sized breath." In this way you become aware of your life. And so you *live* the words of Jesus (and I stress *live* as opposed to *think about*) – "Is not life more than food and the body more than clothing?"

The aesthetic tradition of Japan speaks of just looking, as it speaks of just walking or just sitting or just listening or just doing what you are doing. And all these are variants of just being. Then this tradition comes up with a valuable expression: it speaks of *becoming* the flower or the plant or the bird or whatever. In doing this one loses one's ego and enters into the non-self condition known as *mu-ga*. What precisely this *mu-ga* means (it is a translation of the Sanskrit *anatman*) is much disputed by scholars and need not preoccupy us here. Only let me say that I myself take it to mean that in a flash of enlightenment one loses the illusory and separate ego to find the true or universal self which is open to the universe, open to other people and open to God. The discovery of this true self is indeed a great enlightenment and the door to mystical experience in all the great religions. About it I shall speak more in detail later.

Finally, while I have urged you to pray in the midst of nature with the flowers of the field and the birds of the air, I also urge you to pray in the mighty city. In the swirl and bustle of Fifth Avenue or Ginza or Piccadilly you can pause for a moment to feel the presence of a reality that transcends everything: you can be aware of a world of enlightenment which transcends the phenomenal world that meets your eyes. Teilhard de Chardin was aware of the presence of an all-loving God in the factories and shipyards and airports. God is everywhere and in everything. As you search for him, never forget that he also is searching for you.

SEVEN

✳

Existential Prayer

I have spoken, Thomas, about mystical contemplation and the prayer of just being; and now I would like to lead you further along this path, this privileged path, to which you have been called. But first let me make a new and important distinction: I want to distinguish between **existential** and **essential prayer**. This latter deals with essences. That is to say, it deals with *what* God is and *what* I am. In this prayer you reflect on God's attributes – his goodness and mercy and love; or you reflect on scripture, making use of the words of the sacred text; or you repeat the words of your favourite prayer; or you use your own personal words. In the earlier pages of this book I have proposed many excellent ways of essential prayer, and I suggest that you re-read what I have said.

Existential prayer, on the other hand, is one form of mystical contemplation. It is the prayer of just being. It has few words; and perhaps it has no words at all. It has few images; and perhaps it has no images at all. In this prayer I just *am* – like the flowers of the field or the birds of the air; and by just being I give glory to God.

Now that you have spent considerable time in the practice of essential prayer, Thomas, I see that the time has come for you to allow yourself to be drawn into **existential consciousness**. Now the important thing is not *what* God is but *that* God is; not *what* I am but *that* I am. To practise such prayer you may find it helpful to sit in

56

the lotus posture; but if your knees or back will not take the strain or if you prefer some other posture, feel free. Any posture that appeals to you will do.

As I have said, this is a prayer of silence, without words, without thought, without image, without picture-making. You must simply *be*, with the realization that you are and that God is, without reflection about yourself or about God's attributes or about sacred scripture or about anything holy. The author of *The Cloud* teaches this prayer with consummate wisdom in his beautful little treatise *The Book of Privy Counselling*. I suggest that you take his advice quite literally when he writes:

> When thou comest by thyself think not before what thou shalt do after but forsake as well good thoughts as evil thoughts. And pray not with thy mouth . . . And look that nothing remain in thy working mind but a naked intent stretching unto God, not clothed in any special thought of God in himself, how he is in himself, or in any of his works, but only that he is as he is.

Forsake as well good thoughts as evil thoughts. Get rid of thinking! For that thinking process which was once so precious is now your enemy, a possible source of illusion and an obstacle to that wisdom in emptiness which is the gift of the Spirit and your heart's desire. Alas, a lot of thinking and reasoning may smother the tiny flame of contemplative love that is coming to birth in your heart. So now is the time to abandon thought (even the most beautiful thoughts) in order to practise the prayer of just being and doing nothing.

But let me draw your attention to some important words in the above quotation from *The Book of Privy Counselling*.

The first is that the author speaks of "your working mind", indicating that work and activity are going on, even though you appear to be doing nothing. This shows that he is no quietist advocating a total cessation of activity, but rather is he advocating powerful activity of a different kind.

The second is that the author speaks of a "naked intent stretching out toward God"; and elsewhere he speaks of a naked intent of the will. We know that this English author was a dyed-in-the-wool Thomist, and that when he speaks of a naked intent he means an act of love.

And so when you sit in apparent emptiness and nothingness, when you are just being, when you are in silence and wordlessness – if your contemplation is authentically mystical (and I know, Thomas, that yours is just that) then your being will be filled with a powerfully active love. Yes, at the core of your being is a movement of love, a thrust of love, an unconditional and unrestricted love. There it is, burning brightly; and you are sitting in loving emptiness, in loving nothingness, in loving silence, in loving awareness. And you are now practising not just a prayer of being but a prayer of being in love.

I stress this love, Thomas, since it is the very core of Christian mystical contemplation. The old masters did not permit their disciples to enter into wordless emptiness and silence until this naked intent had come to birth in their hearts. I say *naked intent* but the mystics use other words also. They call it *the blind stirring of love* or *the loving sense of God's presence*. Or they call it *naked faith*. (But note that in this context "faith" means the knowledge born of religious love, so that it is really an admixture of faith and love). Saint John of the Cross in his ecstatic poetry calls it *the living flame of love*, composes a poem to this inner flame and then interprets this phenomenon theologically by stating that the living flame of love is the Holy Spirit. In this way he makes it clear that the whole Christian mystical experience is a work of love, a work of the indwelling Spirit of love.

Again the old masters counsel us to remain at the centre of the soul – also called the *scintilla animae* or the sovereign point of the spirit. For it is precisely here that the flame of love is burning most brightly. And this advice I pass on to you, Thomas. Return to your centre and remain there, not only during your prayer but during your whole day. You will find that as you rest at the centre your whole being is unified in love.

And here let me pause to repeat something that needs repetition. I emphasize the inner movement of love because some people who dabble in mysticism think that to enter mystical contemplation one simply blots out all thinking and all images, makes the mind a blank, becomes totally passive and turns into a zombie. This, of course, is nonsense. The Christian tradition states unequivocally that you may only enter imageless silence when the flame of love or the sense of loving presence are alive in your heart; that is to say, when the naked intent of the will is stretching out towards God.

I have spoken about the inner flame of love, and now let me advance to another point. Love gives birth to a wonderful knowledge which we call "wisdom" in English, *sophia* in Greek and *sapientia* in Latin. This wisdom is not conceptual nor is it accompanied by images: it is not a product of intellectual activity such as reasoning and thinking. It is supraconceptual, obscure, dark, imageless. It is sometimes called unknowing – and the process by which it comes to birth is paradoxically called knowing by unknowing. That is to say, when one no longer knows in images and concepts, supraconceptual knowing or wisdom stemming from love comes to birth. And this is the wonderful wisdom

beside which the discursive knowledge of the scholar is a
tiny candle held up to the glorious light of the noonday
sun.

How happy you are, Thomas, when you practise this
silent contemplation filled with wisdom and love! How
happy you are when you sit, just being – or, more
correctly, just being in love! Now your mind and heart and
whole self are stretching out in love to all men and women,
to the universe and to God. Now you are filled with that
universal love that is the core of the teaching of Jesus. Now
you are possessed by the Spirit of Wisdom who fills the
whole earth.

But you may feel pain because your rational faculties are
emptied and you are in a cloud of unknowing. Not to know
rationally can be frustrating and painful to human nature.
But it is an essential dimension of this kind of prayer. The
old authors spoke of this unknowing when they said that
contemplative love is *blind*. Or they said that this love is
naked, meaning that it is not clothed in thoughts and
images. Indeed, when you enter deeply into this existential
prayer you will find that you *cannot think*, that you cannot
practise discursive meditation, and if you have prepared
material for consideration you may find yourself unable to
concentrate on it. All you want to do is to sit and to be. It
may be that you have a scruple that you are wasting your
time, doing nothing; but rest assured that in this apparent
doing nothing you are in fact doing very much.

And in this existential prayer let me distinguish two
grades.

The first corresponds to Saint Teresa's prayer of quiet.
Here you sit in emptiness and silence, while thoughts float
in and out of your mind. It is as though there were two
layers in your psyche. At one level, a deep level, you are

enjoying the sense of loving presence, while at a more superficial level thoughts are coming and going. When this happens, Thomas, pay no attention to the thoughts floating in and out. Don't try to drive them away (in any case you will be unable to do so) and don't pursue them rationally. This is what the author of *The Cloud* means when he tells you to forsake good thoughts as well as evil ones. Even if beautiful thoughts about God and his love enter your mind, pay no attention to them. You will, of course, see them and you may recognize that they are there – but don't get involved with them. Let them go. Never allow them to withdraw you from that blind stirring of love that burns quietly at the depths of your being. And even if evil thoughts float into your mind, do not fight them. Ignore them. Let them come and let them go. Such is the prayer of quiet.

But there is another stage corresponding to Saint Teresa's prayer of union. Here you are simply held by the sense of loving presence, without any thought or image whatsoever. You are just in deep unitive silence, all thinking, all images, all concepts effectively buried beneath a cloud of forgetting. Usually you will find that this prayer of union does not last long.

The author of *The Cloud* seems to be speaking of some such prayer when he talks about total self-forgetfulness as the apex of mystical experience. He outlines two stages. In the first stage I am conscious that I am and that God is. Just that. But there comes a time when I am forgetful even of my own being and conscious only of the being of God: for the knowledge and feeling of my own being is buried beneath a cloud of forgetting. And this is the peak-point of this author's mystical experience. Here are his words:

> For if thou wilt busily set thee to the proof, thou shalt find when thou hast forgotten all other crea-

tures and all their work – yea! and also all thine own words – that there shall remain yet after, betwixt thee and thy God, a naked knowing and feeling of thine own being: *the which knowing and feeling must always be destroyed* ere the time be that thou mayest feel verily the perfection of this work.

Destroy the naked knowing and feeling of your own being! Clearly the author is here teaching a radically non-objective prayer. All dualism gone, consciousness of God alone remains. The same author is quick to say that to lose one's self in God is a wonderful, gratuitous gift, never the consequence of human effort. Furthermore he goes to great lengths to justify theologically the loss of self; and I shall follow his lead in the chapters that follow.

What I have tried to say in crude and abstract language is described traditionally in a beautiful image based on scripture: that of Mary Magdalene sitting at the feet of Jesus. He loves her, and she loves him. So deep is her love that she is carried beyond all concepts, beyond all words, beyond all images, beyond all reasoning and thinking, into a cloud of unknowing. She is carried beyond his humanity to his divinity, where she rests in loving self-forgetfulness and in silence. If you can pray like Mary Magdalene, Thomas, always do so. Sit at the feet of Jesus and enter into the cloud.

EIGHT

*

Quietism

Let me warn you, Thomas, that if you teach existential prayer or speak about existential consciousness you may find yourself in trouble. Many good, pious, well-meaning people just won't understand what you are talking about. Intelligent, brilliant speculative theologians who revel in rapier-like distinctions will shake sad heads in dismay. People may say that you are navel-gazing and wasting time – both your own time and that of others. The more sophisticated may accuse you of quietism or pantheism or monism or any of the isms that come to hand. They may even write angry letters to Rome, where perplexed prelates will scratch bald heads and consult dreary tomes.

And in these circumstances you may say: "I don't care what people say or think. That's their problem; it's not my problem."

But, Thomas, such an attitude, while in some ways highly admirable, will help neither you nor your critics nor your disciples. Be wise as the serpent and simple as the dove. Find a theological basis for your existential prayer and, having found it, face the world with cheerfulness, self-confidence and compassion. While I myself am convinced that such a theological basis exists I cannot work it out here in ten volumes. Let me simply state a few fundamental principles, leaving the ten-volume work to my declining years.

*

The first danger is quietism. And by this I mean the cessation of all mental activity.

Let me concede that quietism is a real danger. It is taught or encouraged by certain unenlightened dabblers who think that mysticism consists in emptying the mind, becoming blank and turning into a zombie. Beware of such blind guides, Thomas.

But apart from these pseudo-teachers there is the well-known fact that even authentic contemplatives can find themselves wandering off into idleness – literally doing nothing and wasting time. For this reason let me give you some practical advice.

Remember that silent contemplative prayer is the end point of a process. Ordinarily one has to pass through stages of thinking, imagining and talking – through what I have called essential prayer. You will know that the time of contemplation has come by those traditional signs about which I have already spoken. There is, alas, a human tendency to jump to the end point of the process without passing through the preliminary stages. If you make such a jump you may break some bones.

I advise authentic contemplatives who pray silently to have in reserve a word such as "Jesus" or "Mary" or "God" or "love", which they can fall back on. Or I suggest that they return from time to time to awareness of the breathing. In this way they are protected from the danger of idle wandering.

So much for the practicalities. But the fact is that there are times when the authentic mystic seems to be doing nothing, and your task is to make it clear to your critics that this apparent doing nothing is in fact a high form of activity. What you are teaching is not the cessation of all activity but a new kind of activity, silent, powerful and creative.

This is an activity of the deeper powers of the psyche and it is found in various forms all over Asia, from India to Japan. It is found not only in the religious context of yoga and zen but also in the martial arts like judo and karate, as well as in the aesthetic arts like the tea ceremony and the flower arrangement. Let me try to explain this within the context of a modern psychology unknown to the mystical tradition of the medieval West.

We now know that the mind is multi-layered. Ordinarily we live our lives superficially at the top level of reasoning and thinking, talking trivialities, watching television or drinking beer, while the deeper levels of the mind remain dormant or unconscious. These deep levels are, of course, influencing our conduct constantly, and they rise to the surface in our dreams at night.

Now in the Asian arts that I have mentioned, these deeper, ordinarily dormant, forces are awakened and integrated. This is done by a rigorous discipline of body and mind, wherein one is trained in breathing, in sitting, in running and in all kinds of exercises. This training may also include a meditation geared not to anything religious but to the awakening of those same deep subliminal layers of the psyche. One who goes through this training successfully attains to a great inner power sometimes called "one-pointedness" because all the powers of body and mind, conscious and unconscious, are unified, marshalled and concentrated on a single point. The good Asian master, aware of the dangers of quietism, sometimes thunders against idleness and waste of time.

Now in religious meditation (and I am still speaking about Asia) one also attains to one-pointedness, but with a religious dimension – the dimension of faith. In Zen, for example, one goes through a rigorous training of prolonged sitting in the lotus, of abdominal breathing, of meditating on the *koan*, of reciting the sutras; and one is possessed by a radical faith in the universal Buddha nature. Through this discipline and this faith one attains to enlightenment or illumination at the core of one's being.

Christian mystics also attain to a profound one-pointedness; and the Christian tradition had always had its ascetical and mystical training, leading to this end. There is little emphasis, it is true, on breathing and posture (though I feel confident that Christian mysticism of the future will pay attention to these); but monasticism and religious life have assiduously taught what I have called essential prayer, and have given pride of place to liturgy and recitation of the divine office – to the two tables, the table of the word and the table of the eucharist. But above all the Christian tradition has put its chips on the practice of charity – on human love and divine love, even to the shedding of one's blood. This has been the centre of authentic Christian teaching about mystical experience.

It is precisely through the practice of charity in prayer and in life that one attains to Christian one-pointedness. It is precisely through the practice of charity in prayer and in life that the deeper faculties of consciousness are awakened and inflamed. And so the mystics speak of the blind stirring of love, the living flame of love, and so on. For them just being = just being-in-love. The being of the Christian mystic is a great act of love. Could anything be further from cessation of all mental activity? No, Thomas. Properly understood, contemplation shakes the universe, topples the powers of evil, builds a great society, and opens the doors that lead to eternal life.

As the deep subliminal powers are awakened and come into consciousness they impede discursive thinking. At first their action is so subtle and delicate that one may scarcely advert to it and, at this early stage, the mystical powers could be crushed by excessive rational activity. As time goes on, however, they act with more and more power and persistence, so that *one just cannot think*. And it is now that one seems to be doing nothing; it is now that many people fear they are idling and wasting time. Yet it is precisely now that the wise master will tell you not to think but just to be – just to be in this apparent idleness. Follow his advice and you will find that only the top layers of the psyche are doing nothing; the deeper layers are powerfully at work. In authentic Christian contemplation, while the discursive faculties are silenced and put to rest, an immense fire is burning at the core of one's being. The old mystics expressed this poetically with a quotation from "The Song of Songs": "I slept but my heart was awake." One is asleep at the rational level of consciousness; but at the level of the heart one is very much awake.

Moreover, when we understand that the mind is multi-layered, many of the horrendous paradoxes of the mystics fall into place. Take, for example, the talk about knowing and unknowing, about darkness and light, about ignorance and wisdom. All this makes sense when we realize that the mystic does not know at the level of rationality (for this area has been swept clean) but knows at the deeper levels and, above all, at the enlightened centre of the soul. Ignorant at one level, she is wise at another.

But this is not all. The very wisdom that has been awakened is non-conceptual and therefore dark. The fact is that these deeper layers speak a different language, and that is why the mystics speak of dark knowledge and of knowing that is unknowing.

Criticism will not harm you, Thomas. Welcome it. It will force you to think; it will bring you to a deeper understanding; it will purify your practice.

But now let me go on to an even more serious question that is invariably asked: Is this existential, non-objective prayer monistic? or pantheistic? If one enters a silence without subject-object relationship, where is God?

This is indeed an important question to which I shall now address myself.

NINE

✳

Ego, Self, God

Those who practise existential, non-objective prayer sooner or later talk about the loss of self. And this necessarily raises questions about monism and pantheism and those dreadful isms that good people fear. Assuredly, official church documents seldom use words like pantheism and monism. What the Christian community feared was not an ism but any doctrine that might prevent people from calling God Father, any doctrine that would hinder us from crying out: "Abba, Father!" After all, what could be more central to Christianity than the Lord's Prayer? And how can I call on God my Father if I have no self?

Theoretically and theologically this is a formidable question. And yet for people with practical experience of contemplation, the whole thing is a non-problem. The author of *The Cloud* speaks constantly about losing, and even destroying, the knowing and feeling of one's own being. He does not want you to think about your own being or about your self. But note, Thomas, that he never says that your own being does not exist or that your self does not exist. It is one thing to say, "Don't think about your being – don't even be aware of it." It is quite another thing to say, "Your being does not exist" or "Your self does not exist".

For the fact is that the author of *The Cloud*, like any other committed Christian, knows that the key to prayer is love. And we all know that love is ecstatic – it carries us out of ourselves so that our eyes are riveted only on the one we love. When we truly love, we live in the person we love, no longer living in ourselves. And it is about this loving self-forgetfulness that the author of *The Cloud* and all good Christian mystics are talking. When with love we cry out "Abba, Father!" we may forget ourselves in ecstatic union with our Father.

And yet the author of *The Cloud* tries to justify himself further with a Thomistic metaphysic which you may find somewhat obscure. Since I have written a book about this (*The Mysticism of "The Cloud of Unknowing"*), a brief word will be sufficient here.

In Thomistic metaphysics, existence or being is the richest and most all-embracing of notions. When you say that *God is* you have said everything that can be said about God. For this little word "is" includes the fact that God is good and merciful and just and loving: it includes all God's attributes. Put in more technical language, God's existence and his essence are identical: *what God is* and *that God is* are the same. And that is why Aquinas can assert (*pace* the exegetes) that everything that can be said about God is contained in the great formula of "Exodus": "I am who I am." God alone is Being in the full sense of the word.

The consequences for prayer are enormous. When I sit in simple and silent awareness of God's Being, without reflecting on any of his attributes, I am engaging in the richest of all prayers *since all God's attributes are included in his Being*. Is not this a valid justification of existential prayer?

God is the fullness of Being. We, on the other hand, poor humans, are limited being, being by participation. We can even refuse to be, as the anguished Hamlet knew well. "To be or not to be – that is the question." We escape from being when we separate ourselves from God who is the source; we come to the fullness of being when we unite ourselves with God and drink from the source. Separated from God we lack the fullness of being: in God we fully exist. And so the author of *The Cloud* is a true Thomist when he writes that God "is your being and in him you are what you are". God is your being (though you are not God's Being); and in him you become your real self.

The English author then mentions two stages of contemplative prayer. In the first stage I just am. I am and God is. No words, no thinking, no reasoning, no reflecting on God's attributes. This is a prayer of just being. But in it there is still imperfection, since there is some separation between my self and God. The perfection of prayer is reached when I am totally forgetful of self and only aware of God.

I believe, Thomas, that the Thomistic metaphysic is still valid. Nevertheless, I now prefer to take another, more modern approach. So let me begin by distinguishing between the ego and the self.

There is a human tendency to build up or create in ourselves an ego that is separate from other people, separate from the universe and separate from God. And how many millions of people in our existentialist century have suffered intensely from the sense of an isolated, lonely, alienated ego! I could write a book about this, with learned footnotes about Descartes and Sartre and a host of others; but I prefer simply to say here that this notion of a separated self or ego is an illusion. If I think that I am a separate existence I am in illusion.

Thomas Merton expressed it well in his final lecture in Bangkok just before his untimely death by electrocution. In characteristically picturesque language (and in his moments of inspiration Merton *did* write well) he said that Christianity and Buddhism agree that the root of man's problems is that his consciousness is all fouled up and he does not appreciate reality as it fully and really is; that the moment he looks at something, he begins to interpret it in ways that are prejudiced and predetermined to fit a certain wrong picture of the world, in which he exists as an individual ego at the centre of things. And Merton claims that *this experience of ourselves as absolutely autonomous individual egos is the source of all our problems*.

This was Merton's final statement on a problem that greatly dominated the thinking of his last years. Of course he attributes the sense of an absolutely autonomous individual ego to original sin. The separate ego cries out, "I will not serve". In order to lose this illusion of a separate self and to come to the realization of my true self in God I must undergo a great revolution in consciousness – an inner revolution which is for the Christian a *metanoia* or change of heart.

Merton rightly says that this is a point on which Buddhism and Christianity agree; and that calls to my mind a Buddhist meditation that can help us get out of the illusion of a separate ego.

Zen Buddhism speaks of your original face and of "your original face before your parents were born". If we take this as a metaphysical statement about some pre-existing face it might sound absurd. But Zen is not concerned with metaphysics. It is speaking of the unconditioned self, a self that is liberated from all historical and cultural conditioning – even from the mother in whose womb we lay and the father who led us into life. There is a self, Zen Buddhism will claim, that is no longer enchained by all this conditioning – and through silent, non-objective meditation in the lotus we can awaken this true, unconditioned and liberated self.

One way to discover this unconditioned self is to repeat again and again the question: "Who am I? . . . Who am I? . . . Who am I? . . ."; until one fine day (after days or weeks or months or years) I cry out with joy: "**I am!**"

And there are other forms of meditation leading to the same enlightened response. They all help me to discover my original face before my parents were born. And then I realize that I am not what I thought I was. I am not a little, separated, autonomous outsider. I am one with other people, with the universe and with all that is.

I have spoken about losing the illusory ego and discovering the true self. But a basic question still remains: Having found this true self, what is its relationship to God?

Here let me return to the mystics.

Augustine says that God is closer to me than I am to my self, that my being depends on God's presence and closeness. Influenced by Augustine, mystics like Meister Eckhart will say that God is unseparated from all things, for God is in all things and is more inwardly in them than they are in themselves. Saint John of the Cross speaks about the window and the rays of the sun: when the sun is shining brightly and the window is clean you can no longer see the glass but only the rays of the sun; in the same way, in advanced mystical contemplation you can no longer see or experience your self but only God. Saint John of the Cross also speaks of the log of wood and the fire. At first there is separation; but gradually the log is consumed in the flames. Again he says that God communicates his Being "in such wise that the soul appears to be God himself . . . and the soul seems to be God rather than a soul, and is indeed God by participation" (*The Ascent of Mount Carmel* 11:5). Again Saint John of the Cross says that at the beginning of our spiritual journey we see God through creatures but at the end we see creatures through the eyes of God.

From all these sayings (and they could be multiplied) it is clear that the enlightened person goes through periods when he or she has no subject-object relationship with God. It is not a question of "I am here and God is there; and I who am here speak to God who is there". No, no. God is not an object: God is not objectified: he is closer to me than I am to myself. Now there is no separation between myself and God. There is no separate ego. He is closer to me, as the *Koran* says, than my own pulse.

And so, Thomas, do not be afraid to give up reasoning and thinking about God. Do not be afraid to renounce images of God. Do not be anxious when the loving sense of his presence is withdrawn. You may seem to be all alone. It may seem to you that there is no God. You may seem to doubt everything. You may fear that you are becoming an atheist. You may ask why God is silent – if there is a God. You may enter into an existential crisis. You may shout out *Lama Sabacthani!* But gradually you will come to see that your notion of God has been purified – for God is within you and you are not separate from him.

But here let me add a word of caution. Saint John of the Cross says that the soul seems to be God rather than a soul. How true this is – for the soul is the image of God! But it can lead to one of the greatest errors in the spiritual ascent. One who has come to the earthshaking realization of the true self can easily think that he or she has come to the realization of God. In other words one can mistake self-realization for God-realization. Do not make this mistake, Thomas. Never think that you have reached journey's end. Remember that the true self is opening out to the beyond, and that your journey goes on and on and on. It goes beyond the mystery of the self to the mystery of One who knows no limits. Even in eternity we shall never arrive: we shall never exhaust the mystery of God.

The relationship of the true self to God is truly a great and unfathomable mystery, but light is thrown on this problem by the revelation of Jesus who is the Word Incarnate. So let me in the next chapter speak about him.

TEN

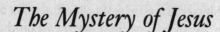

The Mystery of Jesus

People will ask you, Thomas, about the role of Jesus in this existential, non-objective prayer. They will say rightly that Christian prayer must be rooted in the Gospel and, above all, in the Risen Lord. What counts is one's relationship with Jesus and through Jesus with the Father. And the question then arises: Where is Jesus in this silent, existential, imageless, non-objective prayer of just being?

This is indeed an important question to which you must pay careful attention.

Let me begin by saying that in the Christian life you can approach Jesus in many ways:

> You can think about Jesus
>
> You can pray to Jesus
>
> You can pray through Jesus
>
> You can pray with Jesus
>
> You can imitate and follow Jesus
>
> You can allow Jesus to pray within you

All of these ways of prayer will be present in a balanced contemplative life. I urge you to use them all, moving from one to the other under the gentle guidance of the Spirit.

Here I am principally concerned with the inner Jesus:

Jesus who is dwelling within. This is the Jesus of whom Paul can write: "It is no longer I who live, but Christ lives within me" (Galatians 2:20). And the same Paul can say: "For me to live is Christ" (Philippians 1:21), as if to say that Jesus is his very life. This is the Paul who tells us to have the mind of Jesus. The Paul who constantly uses the mystical words "in Christ".

And the indwelling Jesus shines through the pages of the fourth gospel. Here we find the Jesus who dwells in us and we in him and all in the Father. "In that day you will know that I am in my Father, and you in me, and I in you" (John 14:20). Jesus is the vine, the true vine, and we are the branches. He tells his disciples that it is expedient for them that he goes, because if he goes he will send the Spirit. And he will come again in a new way: he will be within them. Indeed, he will be with them every day until the consummation of the world.

And, of course, it is principally through the eucharist that Jesus dwells in the community and in the individual. That is why the eucharist is the very core and centre of Christian life and Christian mystical experience. That is why I have urged you to eat and drink copiously from this rich table. "He who eats my flesh and drinks my blood abides in me, and I in him" (John 6:56). Read again and again the sixth chapter of Saint John and you will understand what I mean.

Remember that through the eucharist Jesus is not simply present within you like water in a glass, when the water and the glass always remain distinct. But through the eucharistic presence you are being transformed into him and, so to speak, becoming him. What an intimate union between you and him is created by the eucharist! The old authors had various picturesque ways of expressing this union. Following the Pauline, "But put on the Lord Jesus Christ . . ." (Romans 13:14), the author of *The Cloud* speaks of being naked of self and clothed with Christ – a fine statement of the non-self condition and the reality of the living Jesus.

The early Christian communities, particularly the Pauline communities and the community of the beloved disciple – were keenly aware of Jesus dwelling in their midst. "That Christ may dwell in your hearts through faith" was the prayer of Paul (Ephesians 3:17); and the indwelling of the risen and eucharistic Jesus was the very basis of a vigorous mystical life that flourished in eastern and western Christianity and remains enshrined in the writing of the Greek and Latin fathers.

But Europe after the Middle Ages moved outwards. It became increasingly preoccupied with discovering continents, conquering peoples, amassing wealth and exploring realities "out there". And religion, always deeply embedded in culture, did not escape this extravertical influence. Religious people fixed their eyes on the outer world, concentrated on cleansing the outside of the cup, strove to conquer worlds for Christ, stressed church membership and statistics, paid great attention to rules and regulations and exterior teachings – as well as to buildings, temporal power and money. Theology became more and more interested in the historicity of the Bible and in the Jesus who lived "back there" before the gospels were written – hence the search for the historical Jesus of Nazareth. And while, it is true, a mystical life never ceased to exist, mystical theology was relegated to a minor place in any theology curriculum. Sermons on contemplative prayer just did not happen.

Lest there be any misunderstanding, let me here say that

I have the highest esteem for those scholars who have devoted their lives to the search for the historical Jesus. Their approach to Jesus "from below", their research on the synoptic gospels, their emphasis on the humanity of the Lord – all this was completely necessary in the twentieth century and has helped immensely our understanding of the gospels. What I am saying is that if this scholarship leads to neglect of the fourth gospel and its teaching that the Word was made flesh and dwelt amongst us, then it will truncate Christian mystical experience, rob us of our mysticism, as well as weaken our dialogue with Hinduism and Buddhism.

Fortunately, however, Western culture kept developing and in this century underwent a *shift to interiority*. Under the influence of Kant and Freud, Jung and Newman, Teilhard and Heisenberg, Western men and women became increasingly aware of inner space and the inner world. They have been driven further within by contact with Hinduism and Buddhism, with their relentless search for the true self. And theology is also undergoing its shift to interiority. Theologians like Rahner and Lonergan became interested in mysticism, in the kingdom within, in the Jesus within, in the interiority of the great religions of the world. My guess is that the theology of the next century (which can in no way neglect Buddhism and Hinduism) will move from the quest for the historical Jesus to the quest for the eucharistic Jesus. And this will bring a flowering of Christian mystical experience.

I have wandered far afield. Let me return to the practicalities of your prayer.

When you receive the eucharist (either actually or spiritually) remember that Jesus is dwelling within you and you in him. It is a real presence. At first you may like to converse with the inner Jesus or to repeat the famous, "Lord Jesus, Son of God, have mercy on me a sinner". But the time may come when you wish to be completely silent and to let Jesus take over. You are, so to speak, permeated by his life and by his presence. Now you begin to understand Paul's "For me to live is Christ . . ." (Philippians 1:21).

In this quiet presence there is a sense of "otherness", and you can easily move from conversation with Jesus to silence and back to conversation. But the time may come when the sense of otherness (and with it the sense of consolation) seems to vanish. And now you are seemingly left alone. Now you are practising non-objective or existential prayer. For Jesus is not objectified. But, Thomas, do not think that he has abandoned you. Far from it. He is hidden. He is so interiorized, so much identified with you, so little objectified that he seems to be absent. You can say with Paul that your life lies hidden with Christ in God.

And this painful sense of absence is an excellent prayer. Remain with it. Do not feel obliged to think about Jesus or to pray to Jesus. Just be! And you will find that Jesus reveals to you the Father who is present, though not objectified, in the depths of your being. This is the Father of whom Jesus said, "I and the Father are one . . ." (John 10:30). This is the Father of whom Jesus said, "The one who has seen me has seen the Father . . ." (John 14:9). This is the Jesus who said, "Believe me that I am in the Father and the Father is in me . . ." (John 14:11).

And so we end with the Trinity. One with Jesus and filled with the Spirit you cry out, "Abba, Father!" Remember that the Holy Trinity is one God. Your prayer has become the prayer of Jesus who is the Word Incarnate.

*

Finally let me return to where I began. I said that a balanced contemplative life contains many approaches to Jesus. I repeat this here. There will be times, perhaps times of anguish, when you must cry out to Jesus with all your heart, "Lord Jesus, Son of God, have mercy on me a sinner". For Jesus is your Saviour.

ELEVEN

---*---

Crisis

I have spoken of the prayer of being, and I have said that this is, in fact, a prayer of being-in-love. If you can pray this way, Thomas, be sure to do so. Yes, abandon good thoughts as well as evil thoughts and enter into the realm of silent and wordless love. Remember that you are on a privileged path. Now you are on the royal road of mystical contemplation. Now you are living the Gospel message of love – or, if you will, of being in love. And the Lord is with you, even when you do not see his face nor hear his voice.

I have already told you that in this silent prayer you may be tempted to think that you are doing nothing or that you are wasting time. But it is only the upper level of your mind, the rational level, that is doing nothing. The deeper, hitherto unconscious levels are surging into ever more powerful activity. These are the levels which, penetrated with faith and love, will be filled with an unearthly wisdom beside which the knowledge of the greatest scholar will seem like consummate ignorance. So let yourself be drawn to the apex of wisdom and allow your true self to be born.

Again I have already said that this seemingly static existential prayer is a journey. It can be compared to the journey through the desert from Egypt to the Promised Land. Or it can be called an inner journey to the depths of one's being. Or it may be a journey into the night. Or it can be compared to that fascinating journey to Emmaus when the two disciples trudged sadly on their way, little knowing that their companion was Jesus – until they recognized him in the breaking of bread.

At first your journey may go smoothly, the sun shining brightly on your path. But sooner or later you will run into turbulence – tempest, rain, mist, earth tremors or whatever. This need not bother you unduly – it is part of the journey. No one promised you a rose garden.

But the time must come when you hit a major crisis which is like an earthquake shaking you to the roots of your being. Such an upheaval may occur two or three times in a lifetime. It is a turning point, a time of growth; and it is important that you recognize it as such.

A crisis may be endogenous. That is to say, it seems to come from within. Quite suddenly and for no apparent reason you awaken at night in fear and trembling, without knowing the cause of your terror or what it is all about. This can be a terrifying experience. You may feel that you are disintegrating or that the framework which upheld your life is collapsing. You may feel a strange presence of evil. Overnight all that gave you security seems to have crumbled, and you know not where to turn. The things that gave you satisfaction no longer do so. You have swings of mood – from elation to depression. You may feel that you are heading for breakdown.

Or the crisis may be triggered off by outer circumstances. You may be crossed in love or rejected by one whom you thought was your friend, and this may shock you profoundly. Or the shock may be failure in your work, or loss of reputation, or humiliation because your weakness or stupidity has appeared before the eyes of all. Or it may be sickness, or loss of a loved one. Whatever it is, you have sleepless nights and anguished days: you find yourself in crisis – in a nosedive or tailspin.

The fact is that your unconscious is rising to the surface. Remember I told you that existential prayer makes an impact on the subliminal levels of the psyche. Remember I told you that deep unconscious forces are at work. Remember I told you that the conscious level is swept clean so that the unconscious can come up. Now it is as though the slender film that separates conscious from unconscious has been ruptured, and the contents of the unconscious are pouring into the conscious mind. All the fears and anxieties and hurts and pains that you have repressed are coming up and filling you with dread. You may be almost overcome with gusts of uncontrollable and irrational anger; there may lurk in your unconscious suicidal tendencies or claustrophobia or agoraphobia or kleptomania or anything. And these tendencies now surface, shattering your sense of security. Something like this is known in Zen where it is called *makyo*, meaning literally "the world of the devil". And the Zen meditator finds himself or herself confronted by all kinds of demons from the unconscious. You, too, may find yourself in this situation and you may ask: What am I to do?

You must find someone to talk to. I do assure you that someone will appear. "When the disciple is ready the master appears" runs the old adage; and this master may be a very unlikely person – someone who is willing to listen and to accept, someone who can reassure you and tell you that you are O.K. Someone who, when you ask, "What am I to do?", can answer, "Do nothing. Just be".

For this is a time when you must do nothing. Let the material from the unconscious come to the surface. Don't fight! Accept! Let the process take place. Learn to integrate; and you will find that gradually (oh, so gradually!) you are becoming a whole person, and the awful split between conscious and unconscious is being healed. Yes, beneath all those demons from the unconscious, the true self is coming to birth – the true self which is like a pearl of great price or a treasure hidden in a field. During the crisis you may have difficulty in believing this. But, believe me, it is true.

Let me look more carefully at the material that is pouring into your conscious mind, causing such frightful suffering.

First there is your shadow. For, Thomas, we all have our shadow: that part of our personality that we have not accepted and that we hate to see. This shadow may come to the surface in frightening dreams. It may be that you see an intruder banging on your door, smashing it down and trying to enter. What a fearful fellow! But happy are you if you can share this dream with an understanding person who will tell you to welcome that intruder in fantasy and to make him your friend. And so for other figures in your dreams.

And then there is your sexuality. You know that we all have in our unconscious a contra-sexual figure. You have your *anima* just as the woman has her *animus*. And now your sexuality will rise to the surface of consciousness in dreams at night and upheavals during the day. This is a time when some people discover that they are still bogged down in the Oedipus conflict, or that they are still passion-ately attached to father or mother. And again you must accept and integrate this sexuality (or, more correctly, let integration take place; for the process is going on and you simply have to let it go on); for it is through the union of the conscious and the unconscious mind that you will find wholeness and come to individuation. Indeed, through all this suffering an interior marriage is taking place between your *anima* and your *animus*; and when this marriage happens you are a whole person.

Again, there will be the problem of your mask. Yes, Thomas, you wear a mask when you identify with your role of teacher or doctor or priest or father or writer or whatever. Or you stand on your pedestal, gloriously inflated before the world. And now, during this crisis, the mask is torn from your face and you are revealed as you truly are. You are knocked off your pedestal and find yourself in the dust with the rest of men. This is terribly painful but it is the road that leads to the joyful discovery of your true self – without mask and without pedestal. What joy you will have when you discover your original face before your father and mother were born!

When all the garbage of the personal unconscious has come to the surface there eventually rises the deeper archetypal shadow from the collective unconscious. Now you are confronted by death and by existence itself. But about this I will speak later, when I treat of existential dread. Enough to say here that in Jungian terms this is a developmental crisis – an adult developmental crisis – painful indeed but a necessary part of the journey. Jung himself went through such a crisis and he called it his confrontation with the unconscious. It was a major step forward in the path to fullness of personality which he called individuation.

I have said that you must find a friend or counsellor. Now let me add (and remember this when you are directing others) that you must view the situation in a holistic way. That is to say, you must see a psychological, a religious and a physical dimension to your situation.

There is a **psychological dimension**: the rising of the unconscious and of the memories and fears of your life back to the womb. These will flow into your conscious mind. And in order to handle this material from the unconscious it may be necessary to meet a professional counsellor – to speak about your childhood, your relationship with father and mother, your sexuality, your hang-ups with authority and the rest. All this will help you to cope so that integration may take place.

But preoccupation with the psychological must not blind you to the **religious dimension** of what is happening. For the fact is that in such a crisis (be it in yourself or in others) you are face to face with the unfathomable mystery of the human person and the mind-boggling mystery of existence. Psychology may help; but psychology will not save you. Jesus is your saviour and you need faith in him. You are like those disciples rowing desperately in the boat and crying out in panic when they see Jesus walking on the waters. Imitate them. Cry out to Jesus. Or you are like those same disciples who were filled with fear of the swelling seas while Jesus slept. Don't worry. He will wake up and calm the storm. Trust in him. Instinctively, Thomas, you will turn to him. This is a time when you clutch your crucifix with great love and with many tears. "Lord Jesus, Son of God, have mercy on me a sinner."

Yes, you will find that you need a Saviour and you will call on the Lord. But this is not a time for prolonged prayer. Probably you will be unable to kneel or to sit in the lotus for long periods of time. You may find it more helpful to take long walks or to work in the fields or in the garden, just letting the inner process take place. And, of course, you will be happy to eat from the table of the eucharist. Here you will find food for your journey.

But besides a psychological and religious dimension there is also a **physical dimension**. For the body will share in your crisis. It may be that you become exhausted, that you suffer from insomnia or high blood pressure or ulcers, or that you have bouts of depression or any of those sicknesses that come from stress. All this is part of your crisis – it is the crisis of the body. So attend to your health. Remember I told you to take fresh air, exercise and good food. Don't neglect to do this now. Deep breathing you will also find helpful. If the doctor prescribes medicine, take it. If he prescribes a vacation, take that. But beware of chemicals – I don't say that you should avoid them completely, but beware.

And beware also of reductionism.

Your friends will say that you are "tired". Of course you are tired but that is only part of your problem.

Or they will say you need psychotherapy or counselling. And of course you do need counselling and perhaps psychotherapy; but psychology alone will not solve your problem.

Or they will tell you to pray with total trust. And of course you must pray. But prayer alone will not solve your problem.

What I am saying is that you must view your crisis in a holistic way, as a crisis of body, psyche and spirit. And then, while taking all the human means at your disposal, put your trust in God. In the old days we said, "Trust in God". Now I hear people say, "Trust in the process". I have nothing against that; for it is God's process.

It is interesting to watch crisis in the lives of great people. Think of Paul on the road to Damascus – the blinding light, brighter than the noonday sun; the voice of Jesus; and Paul, shocked and blind, neither eats nor drinks for three days. To the Arabian desert he goes; and this Paul, who has suffered the loss of all things, takes a totally new direction in life. Saul died and Paul was born.

Towards the end of the first book of *The Dark Night* Saint John of the Cross describes a mystical crisis. He speaks of the psychic upheavals that necessarily come to those people who will enter the second night. Sexuality rebels (he speaks of the demon of fornication) while scrupulosity, anxiety and fear surge into consciousness. Temptation to blaspheme and curse God rise up. And such a crisis lasts a longer or shorter time according to the degree of purification to be effected. Ordinarily it will last for several years. It is the prelude to entrance into that night of the spirit which, strictly speaking, is the real mystical path.

Then there is the remarkable Swedish mystic, Emanuel Swedenborg. In his fifty-fifth year he passed through an earthshaking crisis which lasted for two years and transformed his life. He woke up at night with fear and trembling; he had strange and bizarre dreams as well as waking visions. Several times he was hurled across the room and heard loud noise as of thunder. Some people have said he was crazy: others maintain that his unconscious erupted violently. He himself called this crisis his entry into the spirit world; and, when it was over, he devoted the rest of his life in a balanced way to the study of the Bible and to the things of the spirit.

From these examples (and they could be multiplied) you will see, Thomas, that this crisis is a time of death and resurrection. The framework that upheld one's life collapses, leaving one adrift on a sea of insecurity. But in the midst of this turmoil comes the call: "Samuel, Samuel . . ." One is called to something new.

It is interesting to note that modern psychology talks more and more about life cycles and a journey, and to this I will now turn.

TWELVE

———————— ✳ ————————

Second Journey

It is interesting to note that modern psychology frequently compares life to a journey, and recently we have heard more and more about a second and a third journey – and then about a final journey which is death. It is as though human life passes through several cycles in which the same person has new values, new ideals, a new orientation – in which he or she is a new person. Now that the life span has increased dramatically such new journeys are becoming a normal part of human living.

And here I want to say that the crisis you have passed through is the beginning of your new journey. A page has been turned in the book of your life. You will look back and reflect: "Until now I lived on the surface of life, little realizing the depths and depths that lie beneath." Now you will realize that, like Peter, you are launching out into the deep, into unknown and unchartered areas of your psyche and spirit where you will catch innumerable fish. A new life is beginning.

The crisis I have described will come to an end gradually. Remember I told you that the unconscious is surfacing and your true self is being born. This true self is very beautiful; but in rising up, it brought with it all kinds of garbage and crud – and this has caused you trouble. But gradually you will learn to cope. Gradually you will learn to accept. Gradually you will learn to integrate. And peace, deep peace, a peace that the world cannot give, floods your mind and body and spirit. But do not think that the process is over. The crisis may be over; but the process is not. You will never be free from storms. Only now you have learnt to accept – and to smile.

I have said that your true self is coming to birth. Now let me add that the Rhineland mystic Eckhart, following an ancient mystical tradition, speaks of the birth of God in the soul. And I tell you that not only your true self but the very Word of God is coming to birth in you. That is why you can cry out with Paul, "It is no longer I that live but Christ lives in me". That is why you can say with Paul, "For me to live is Christ . . ." You are becoming more and more filled with the presence of one who loves you and gave himself up for you.

However, your journey is only beginning and I must give you some instruction about what you should and what you should not do. But remember that I cannot give you a map. With Saint John of the Cross, prince of Christian mystics, I tell you that to go to a place you do not know you must go by a way that you know not. You know neither the way, nor the goal. God alone knows where you are going – and how. But, on the other hand, it is also true that mystical language is full of paradox; and there is a sense in which you *do* know the way and the goal. You know by unknowing. You know by denying your ordinary knowledge and living by dark faith.

The mystical journey has two aspects, which I like to express in terms of Chinese philosophy. There is **the way of personal effort** and **the way of non-action,** known in Chinese as *wu-wei*. Let me speak briefly about these two ways.

The way of personal effort is what the words say. It is the way in which you work and do your part: you labour and sweat and toil. This way begins with a great resolution, a great determination. Here you can learn much from the Zen people who stake their lives on their practice, declaring that even if they die they will go through to enlightenment. And you, too, must make a mighty resolution to go over mountain and ocean in search of your beloved, plucking no flowers and fearing no wild beasts.

Concretely, this is a resolution to follow Jesus in his life and in his death, to follow him to Gethsemane and to Golgotha and to Galilee. And in order to do this you must read the gospels again and again and again until they come alive within you, penetrating the subliminal levels of your mind and rendering you one with Jesus. Above all, the cross of Jesus must be constantly before your eyes.

Pay special attention to those parts of scripture that speak of the demands of discipleship. The one who does not renounce all possessions cannot be the disciple of Jesus. The kingdom of heaven is like a treasure buried in a field: a man sold everything he possessed (and note that everything does mean everything, and that he did this with great joy) in order to buy that field. To be the disciple of Jesus you must hate father and mother, yea, and your own life also. You must take up your cross and follow Jesus. No need for me to give a list of such passages. Only let me say that you must be completely emptied and radically poor.

And don't neglect the apostle to the Gentiles. Make your own that passage in Philippians where Paul is running like an athlete in the Greek games: "that I may know him and the power of his resurrection, and may share his sufferings, becoming like him in his death, that if possible I may attain the resurrection from the dead" (Philippians 3:10). What a magnificent description of the race you are now in! It passes through the suffering of Jesus to his joyful resurrection from the dead.

You know that in Zen Buddhism the way of personal

effort is concretized in a very powerful discipline known in Japanese as *gyo*. Remember that in the Christian way the most important *gyo* is love of neighbour. In this is everything contained. Read the authentic mystics and you will find them saying: "Mysticism is love. No love: no mysticism." So be sure that human love penetrates your life and that it keeps growing and growing. No need to tell you that there are many kinds of love, and that all play a crucial role in your life of prayer. There is the tender love of the Good Samaritan by which you go out in compassion to the sick and the afflicted, the oppressed and the lonely. There is the love for the community by which you wash the feet of the brethren – and you must always remind married people that love for their family is their royal road to mysticism. Then there is the love of friendship, a love that leads to intimacy and mutual indwelling. Such love has played a central part in the lives of outstanding mystics.

And here let me pause to point to a strange paradox (or should I say aberration?) in the lives of some good, would-be mystics. They have thought that they should insulate themselves from human love in order to practise heroic detachment. What a strange misreading of the Gospel! They have thought that the deep involvement, the inner turmoil and the sleepless nights that often accompany authentic love would be an obstacle to their tranquil life of prayer. Do not fall into this error. It is true that authentic human love may tear out your guts; but the emptiness of the lover is precisely his or her way to enlightenment.

And needless to say there is the table of the eucharist about which I have already spoken constantly. This is the *agape*, the banquet of love.

So much for the way of personal effort.

*

Together with the way of personal effort you must practise **the way of non-action** or *wu-wei*. In this way your prayer becomes more and more effortless. For this is the way of surrender or abandonment. In Chinese philosophy one surrenders to the powers of the universe and to the subliminal powers of the psyche. One does not interfere (and for this reason it is sometimes called the way of non-interference) nor does one fight against nature. How often I have told you, Thomas, to let the process take place, let growth take place, let nature act! And, of course, this is agonizing because it means that you give up your desire to control, your desire to be master of your own life, your desire to make plans.

In your case, Thomas, as with every Christian, you are surrendering to the action of a loving God whom you believe to be the author of all that happens in the universe and in your life. Yes, you surrender to the Spirit. And in this you will find a wonderful model in the Virgin Mary who uttered her earthshaking *fiat*: "Behold, I am the handmaid of the Lord; let it be to me according to your word" (Luke 1:38). It is as though she said: "Let the process take place. I know that I am chosen; I know that I am loved; I know that I am full of grace. So now I surrender to your love and I will put no obstacle in the way." If the spirit of the *fiat* permeated the whole life of Mary (and I believe it did) then we can look to her as the greatest contemplative of all time.

And as you surrender to the Spirit you will find that you must let go – let go, let go, let go of all that has given you security. You must let go of all those needs the consumer society has created in you. And not only that. You must let go of attachment to health, to reputation, to possessions. Even more painful – you must let go of attachment to friends, to work, to longing for recognition. And as you let go of all that gave you security, you will feel an awful insecurity, as though you were disintegrating psychologically and even physically. There may be times when you feel you are falling apart.

As you let go, you are advancing further and further into the unknown. In order to go to a place you do not know, you must go by a way that you know not. And this can be, oh, so frightening. You may feel very lonely: and again you may wake up at night trembling with fear. But do not let this stand in your way. Accept the fear! Do not fight it! It will give way to peace – or, more correctly, it will become peaceful. For your sorrow will be turned into joy.

In these circumstances you may grasp desperately at some bauble, like a drowning man clutching at a straw. But this bauble will not help you. It may even torture you. You must simply let go: there is no alternative. Let me express it in another way.

You are starting out on a journey and you must say goodbye. You will have to say goodbye constantly – to everyone and to everything. It is a radical farewell. "Goodbye! I'm going on a journey. Goodbye, father and mother and brethren and wife and family and friends and lands. Goodbye, structures and rules and regulations that gave me security. Goodbye, states of prayer that gave me joy. Goodbye, doctrines and dogmas that made everything seem so clear and certain. Goodbye! I'm venturing out into the deep with no land in sight and no other light save the love that burns in my heart." This is the *nada, nada, nada* which will ring in your ears.

To say goodbye to what you see and hear and touch is one thing. Even more painful is your farewell to the figures in your unconscious, to the memories to which you have been clinging. As the process goes on you will find (without perhaps knowing what is happening) that you are saying goodbye to memories. Perhaps, after many decades of separation, you are only now saying goodbye to father and mother, to the memories of childhood and of your whole life. This is a radical farewell; and you will feel deep grief. If tears come to your eyes, let them fall. Weep abundantly as you say goodbye. These tears should have fallen decades ago. Only now are they streaming down your cheeks. So let them come. This is a wonderful purification of your memory; and it will make you free. Yes, a great liberation will ensue.

When with tears and anguish and pain you have said goodbye to everything you will find that you have lost nothing. You have not said goodbye to your friends: you have said goodbye to clinging and attachment to your friends. You have not said goodbye to memories: you have said goodbye to clinging and attachment to memories. You have not said goodbye to the good things of this world: you have said goodbye to clinging and attachment to the good things of this world. You have not said goodbye to knowing and rationality; you have said goodbye to clinging and attachment to knowing and rationality. You have not said goodbye to doctrines and dogmas: you have said goodbye to clinging and attachment to doctrines and dogmas. And so for all good things. Now you can resonate with Paul who wrote: "Finally, brethren, whatever is true, whatever is honourable, whatever is just, whatever is pure, whatever is lovely, whatever is gracious, if there is any excellence, if there is anything worthy of praise, think about these things" (Philippians 4:8) For all things are yours; and you are Christ's; and Christ is God's.

This is enlightenment. Liberated from addictions and enslaving needs (yes, even those which dwelt in your unconscious and tortured you), you will gradually come to an inner freedom that brings intense joy. You will experience moments or periods of joy like that man who sold everything to buy that field in which lay buried the treasure. Or yours will be the joy of the merchant who found a pearl of great price: the joy of all those strange and beautiful people who laughed when they possessed nothing – only God. Their security was in having no security. You will find that you are becoming more spontaneous, more human, more alive. Now you can laugh and cry and sing and dance without those constricting inhibitions that formerly cramped your style. For now you have become your true self. In losing the little, separate ego you have found the true self which is one with the flowers of the field and the birds of the air, one with the poor and the sick and the suffering, one with the universe, one with God himself.

And now you can love. You can love father and mother and brethren and wife and family – even your own life you can love. You may find that for the first time you are capable of authentic friendship. For now you love your friends not for the security they give you but for what they are in themselves. Now you may find that you love everyone you meet in the street or on the bus. Like Paul you have become all things to all men and women.

And you will experience a wonderful flowering of your personality, as unexplored and untapped potential rises to the surface of consciousness. That mask by which you identified with your role was limiting you, making you wretchedly narrow. Now that you have cast it away, other talents come to the fore – talents you never dreamed you possessed. You have blossomed and become a richer person. You rejoice in that wisdom beside which the knowledge of the scholar looks like ignorance.

And as you become your true self you will find that you are strangely indifferent to public opinion and to what people say and think. If formerly you were a drifter who went along with the crowd, saying and doing what the masses say and do, now you will find that you stand apart as your unique self. And, of course, that will get you into trouble. Yes, Thomas, when the chips are down, any institution, be it church or state or college or religious order, feels uncomfortable with the person who is himself, thinks for himself and says frankly what he thinks. Such a person stands out like a sore thumb. Such a person is a misfit.

The Carmelite mystics (Teresa and John) say clearly that one who sets out on this path can expect trouble, and that a man's enemies are those of his own household. So you must learn to accept criticism – "that's their problem, not mine" – and realize that, like the prophets, you may be put to death. But if so, you will die with a smile.

I have outlined the spark of enlightenment that will come to you. But I told you before and I tell you again: never think you have reached journey's end. Never think that you have arrived. Keep climbing the mountain, and remember that wise and gentle lady who responded clearly to her young disciple's questions:

"Does the road wind uphill all the way?"
"Yes, to the very end."
"Does the day's journey take the whole long day?"
"From morn till eve, my friend."

As you climb up that road you will have more crises and storms. Having put your hand to the plough, don't turn back, even though the road winds up and up and up.

But let me give you one more model or paradigm, one symbol or picture to illustrate what I am saying. The model is Jesus himself.

In the ninth chapter of Saint Luke, Jesus sets his face to

go to Jerusalem, and the remaining chapters of this gospel centre around that great journey, which is his second one. It leads to Jerusalem where Jesus meets his death and resurrection. And in this way Jesus becomes himself. As Paul writes so well: ". . . designated Son of God in power according to the Spirit of holiness by his resurrection from the dead, Jesus Christ our Lord . . ." (Romans 1:4). It is as though Paul were saying that through death and resurrection (which John calls his glorification) Jesus became his true self – became what he was from the beginning. And Jesus is your model. Your second journey, Thomas, is leading to Jerusalem – to death and resurrection. You must see it as such. Never banish the thought of death from your consciousness. Look forward to death as the last stage in growth, the last stage of the process; and pray constantly for the grace to die well. Open your arms to the lady death: "Welcome, Sister Death!" Yes, the time will come – soon, all too soon – the call to that last journey when you pass from this world to the Lord, in whose Father's house there are many mansions. Come, Lord Jesus! Come!

THIRTEEN

Return to Paradise

I have tried to say that one who would enter deeply into mystical contemplation must necessarily pass through crisis and embark on a second journey. I have also said that one can distinguish two aspects of this journey: *the way of personal effort* and *the way of non-action*. In the way of personal effort one works and toils: in the way of non-action one surrenders to the action of grace.

Again, I have said that one can only describe this mysterious journey in symbolical terms, and now I would like to propose for your consideration a series of symbols used by the desert fathers and occupying an important place in patristic theology. I refer to the theme of *the return to paradise* or *the recovery of paradise*. Put quite simply, the monks who, in the fourth and fifth centuries of the Christian era, went into the Egyptian desert to live a life of solitude, poverty and virginity, were motivated by the desire to return to the Garden of Eden – not to an earthly paradise but to an inner garden of holiness. Born in *the state of original sin* they strove to return to *the state of original justice*.

This theme is for me all the more interesting in view of an inspiring dialogue between a Buddhist and a Christian. The monk Thomas Merton and the Zen scholar Dr D. T. Suzuki focus on the Genesis story as an important link in the dialogue between Buddhism and Christianity. They find parallels between the stories of the Zen masters and those of the desert fathers; they find parallels between the poverty of the Christians and the emptiness of the Buddhists, between the wisdom of Christianity and the *prajna* of Buddhism; and they discuss such terms as purity of heart, innocence, suchness and knowledge. What is most interesting is their discovery that the Zen monk who went in search of enlightenment and the Christian monk who went in search of holiness – the Christian returning to the state of original justice and the Zen monk searching for his original face – were on very similar paths and had much in common. But let me first speak of the story itself.

The man and the woman were created in the image of God. It was not man alone nor woman alone but man-and-woman who formed the divine image. And this image was untarnished in such wise that they lived in harmony with God, in harmony with the universe, in harmony with one another. They had no fear of the wild animals, which Adam had called by name. They had no fear of death. They had no fear of God, with whom they walked in harmonious friendship. They were, moreover, naked and unashamed, since their sexuality was integrated, as were their other drives and passions; and they were liberated from what was later called concupiscence.

In short, the man and the woman were truly human, in touch with their true selves and united with God. They are symbols of human nature in its ideal state; and the scholastics were to call their condition the *state of integrity* or *the state of innocence* or *the state of holiness*. Saint Thomas Aquinas did not hesitate to say that Adam was a mystic who knew God "without mean" (*sine medio*). Not that Adam possessed the beatific vision but that he knew God without reasoning from the sensible world. His knowledge of God was infused; and he enjoyed the sense of presence that characterizes the life of so many mystics. Such was the state of original justice.

But then came the serpent and the temptation to eat the forbidden fruit of the tree of the knowledge of good and evil. The subsequent sin shocked the man and the woman to the roots of their being, as it shocked the whole wide universe in which they lived. The main consequence of the sin was *separation*. They are separated from God in such wise that they are filled with fear and anguish; and they hide themselves. They are separated from one another in such wise that they are ashamed of their nakedness. They are separated from the earth, which is cursed. And they are separated from their true selves, inwardly broken and shattered – filled with anguish and with concupiscence. They are separated from paradise: the way to the tree of life is guarded by a flaming sword which turns every way. Such is the state of original sin.

And now the question arose in the minds of Christians: Is it possible to return to paradise? Is it possible to recover the state of original justice? Saint Paul hints that such a return is possible. And the monks went into the desert with this intention. There are stories of their friendship with wild animals; but this is very, very secondary. What they really wanted was friendship with God. What they wanted was the holy state of union with God, with the human family, with the universe – and union within themselves. They knew that they could only find these things through the grace of Jesus who is the second Adam and leads to life. Through one man came sin into the world and through one man came liberation from sin. But let me return for a moment to a Buddhist who throws some light on the condition resulting from original sin.

Dr D. T. Suzuki is deeply interested in the tree of the knowledge of good and evil. He claims that in eating the fruit and acquiring the knowledge of good and evil, the man and woman fell into discursive thinking or, in his terms, into the use of the discriminating intellect. *And this is ignorance.* And before eating the forbidden fruit they were without discursive thinking and in harmony with all – *and this is wisdom.* Put bluntly he equates scientific knowledge with ignorance, and wisdom with innocence: he believes that scientific knowledge divides whereas contemplative wisdom unites. This is an interesting insight, showing how profoundly he would sympathize with Richard of St Victor's contention that when contemplation is born reason dies. Perhaps in a radical way (not to be taken literally, for Suzuki was not a man to reject science and scholarship) he is simply asserting the superiority of the contemplative life – which has a wisdom beside which the knowledge of the scholar seems like ignorance.

As you know, my intention in these pages is primarily practical. This is no speculative treatise in theology but a handbook of solid food for your journey. So let me again focus on the practicalities.

From the model of return to paradise it will be clear that your second journey begins with a turning away from sin. It begins with a *metanoia* or change of heart. The cruel crisis through which you have passed was such a *metanoia*: through it you came to repudiate certain tendencies that were blighting your life. In your unconscious there had perhaps been addictions or inclinations that were separating you from God, from other people and from your true self. And now the separate ego is dying (thanks to the sufferings you have undergone) and the big self is coming to birth.

But you must never forget that you have an inbuilt inclination to sin, an inbuilt tendency to build up the separate ego. Acknowledging this you must turn to God in trust. You are the prodigal who, returning to his father's

house asking to be treated as a servant, finds the fatted calf
sizzling merrily on the grid. But it is always possible to run
away again. However profound your enlightenment, never
think that you are unlike the rest of men. Remember how
Jesus said: "I saw Satan fall like lightning from heaven"
(Luke 10:18). The greater the enlightenment, the more
disastrous the fall.

And so the old masters stressed, above all, humility: the
recognition of your own weakness. But what is this
humility?

Modern people are much preoccupied (and rightly so)
with personal responsibility and human dignity. They
cannot accept the humility that is weak subservience:
becoming a doormat to be walked on. Joining hands with
the Buddhist, we must rethink our notion of humility,
seeing it as total emptiness and total poverty. Pride builds
up our ego, separating us from God and man and woman;
humility makes us lose this separate ego to find a true self
united with God and man and woman. It is true that in the
Christian life charity is the queen of virtues; but without
emptiness and loss of this separate ego, how can there be
charity?

Practically, you will move towards humility by emptying yourself and saying goodbye to everything as I have
already counselled you. Yes, empty yourself of everything
– and everything means everything. Let that mind be in
you which was in Christ Jesus, who emptied himself taking
the form of a slave. If anyone takes your coat, give him
your cloak as well. If anyone strikes you on one cheek, turn
the other. If anyone obliges you to walk one mile, walk
two. Give to everyone without asking in return. Then you
will be empty, and you'll know that the road winds uphill
all the way, yes to the very end.

Empty yourself of reasoning and conceptualization and
discursive thought. Get rid of all anxieties. Empty yourself

of your cherished plans, your towering ambitions and your love for your darling projects. Cast from your face that mask! Get off your pedestal! What a fool you'll become! And you'll be foolishly smiling and laughing in situations which formerly made you gnash your teeth with rage. For now you are free. And what a gift is inner freedom!

You will find that you have lost your fear of death. With Paul you will cry out: "O death where is thy sting? O grave, where is thy victory?" (1 Corinthians 15:55). It isn't that you have reasoned yourself into this fearlessness. It is just that you wake up one fine morning and you laugh and laugh – for death is no longer a black ogre but the sweet sister whom you love.

And need I say that Jesus, the second Adam, is your Saviour and your guide? You have learned to clutch your crucifix with great joy. But while you love your crucifix you also know that the risen Jesus is waiting for you in the garden. Yes, the old Adam has disappeared and, behold, in the garden you find Jesus, as Mary Magdalene found him; and he said, "Mary" and she replied "Rabboni" which means master. That was a wonderful meeting in a wonderful garden. You will meet Jesus in the same way, and you'll say: "The road winds uphill all the way. But it's a magnificent road!"

Soon you will be so united with Jesus that he will be in you – no longer objectified. Now you are one with Jesus, one within yourself, one with all men and women, one with the Father. Contemplation which – in the words of *The Cloud* – is a one-ing exercise that has led you beyond all divisions.

But again I return to the old warning. Never think you have reached journey's end. The tree of good and evil is there, and the fruit looks delicious; the slimy serpent can always raise his shining head; concupiscence is never completely dead. So while you rejoice, work out your salvation in fear and trembling.

In the dialogue with Suzuki, Merton is enthusiastic about the similarities between the Zen masters and the monks in Egypt. But he points to two significant differences. One is that, while in the Christian path the notion of personality is highly developed and stress is laid on the uniqueness and richness of each individual human person, this notion seems to be unknown in Zen. It is not that personality is non-existent among Buddhists. It is indeed present in a big way. But the notion of personality is not developed. Merton concludes that the strongly personalistic tone of Christian mysticism seems to prohibit a full equation with Zen experience.

The second difference is more important. For the Christian monk the recovery of paradise is not journey's end but only the beginning. The desert father John Cassian distinguishes between an intermediate end and an ultimate or final state in the life of the monk. The intermediate end is purity of heart and inner poverty, together with a deep sense of God's presence known through unknowing – that is to say, through the abandonment of conceptual thinking. This is the innocence lost by Adam and in some measure found by the monk. On the other hand, the ultimate and final state lies beyond death in the resurrection and eschatological realities of The Book of Revelation.

Reflect carefully on this, Thomas. Return to Eden. Enjoy its luscious beauty. But do not stay there. You will only reach the fullness of enlightenment through death and resurrection.

*

Let me add one corollary. Saint Paul speaks of Jesus as the new Adam. The Church fathers speak of Mary as the new Eve. Death came through Eve and life through Mary. As you return to some measure of integrity, recall the presence of Mary who spent her life in the state of holiness.

FOURTEEN

*

Existential Dread

I have already spoken about the crisis which must inevitably come if your path to mystical contemplation is to reach fruition. The shadow side of your personality will come to the surface, and all the repression that has been in your personal unconscious since childhood will rise in rebellion, so that you find yourself overcome with fear and anxiety, with anger and lust and you know not what. This is a painful experience. But through acceptance and integration, through the realization that your shadow is your friend, you come to a certain maturity and wholeness; you come to a discovery of your true self in all its richness.

But besides a personal unconscious you have a collective unconscious. This is the archetypal part of the psyche in which lies not your personal shadow but the existential shadow. Here lie archetypes and symbols and images of a wider, collective nature. And as your journey goes on, sooner or later, as surely as night follows day, the deeper realms of the psyche must rise to the surface, giving you greater joy and greater distress than you experienced in your former crisis.

Yes, sooner or later, you come face to face with raw existence. If previously you were anxious about your health or your reputation or your work or your relationships, now you feel deep anxiety about your very existence. It is as though your very existence was threatened and in doubt. Listen to the good author of *The Cloud*:

All men have matter of sorrow; but most especially
he feeleth matter of sorrow that knoweth and
feeleth *that he is*. All other sorrows in comparison
with this be but as game to earnest. For he may
make sorrow earnestly that knoweth and feeleth not
only *what he is* but *that he is*. And whoso felt never
this sorrow, let him make sorrow; for he hath never
felt perfect sorrow.

And the author continues with a picturesque description of
the poor disciple slumping in his chair, sobbing and
exhausted, telling him to exercise discretion in such wise
that he strains neither body nor spirit. It is indeed a
remarkable description of the awful burden and anguish of
existence – of what I call existential dread.

The English poet T. S. Eliot wrote that humankind
cannot bear too much reality. And with these words he hit
the nail on the head. Humankind just cannot bear too
much reality. Poor people, we cannot stand the immense
weight of existence and so, ordinarily, we run away to
baseball or beer or billiards or bread. Or we turn to frenetic
activity. But we cannot run away for ever. And you
especially, who have chosen this contemplative path, will
be unable to escape. The time will come when you must
come face to face with naked existence.

And existence without essence is unlimited. It goes on
and on and on without end. It may seem like emptiness or
nothingness. I have said that this crisis involves the archetypal area of the psyche and that the great symbols from
the collective unconscious are rising to the surface. Now
let me add that one of the most important and shattering
symbols of the unconscious mind is *nothing*. Such is the
doctrine of the whole apophatic tradition of Western mysticism. Such is the doctrine of *The Cloud* which speaks
quaintly of "alling and noughting". Such is the doctrine of
Saint John of the Cross who beats the drum on *nada*. Such

is the doctrine of Zen and the apophatic tradition of Asia. As one penetrates more and more deeply into reality one comes face to face with a wall of nothingness, emptiness, void. One is filled with great doubt and great fear. One may feel that one is looking into hell. And this may take the concrete form of a shattering momentary experience when one finds oneself saying "I am", where this "I" is alone, isolated, timeless and awake for ever. What a terrible experience! Yet most mystics have gone through something like this.

I say most mystics; but the experience is profoundly human and is not limited to the mystical path. All humans have a capacity for existential dread; but most people push their fear to a slot at the back of the mind where it lies dormant. Perhaps we have a built-in psychic defence mechanism which prevents our dread from surfacing and lets us carry on with the business of living. Or, as I have said, we brush it aside with baseball or beer. But the time will come when we can no longer run away. Perhaps it will be at the time of death – or when news comes that we have some terminal illness. Or it may come at a time of shock or stress when we are thrown for a loop by the slings and arrows of outrageous fortune. To be or not to be – that is the question. Existence is the question. Traditionally we have spoken of the four last things: death, judgement, hell and heaven. These are deeply human and existential archetypes that must sooner or later rise up before the mind's eye.

Now you may wonder why the experience of existence should be so terrible. After all, is not existence benevolent? Is not existence equal to God? Surely this is the Thomistic understanding of "I AM" or "I AM WHO I AM" in the Book of Exodus. And if God is infinitely good and merciful why should we cringe in shattering fear when we meet him face to face?

This is a good question. To answer it let me return to *The Cloud*. When the author speaks of the intense sorrow of the man who knows that he is, he is speaking of the sorrow of the man who knows that *he is as he is*. In other words he is speaking of the man who knows that he is a sinner and, in consequence, separated from God. He is speaking of the man who exclaims with Adam: "I heard the sound of thee in the garden, and I was afraid, because I was naked; and I hid myself" (Genesis 3:10). Yes, you, too, will pass through a time of existential dread when you hide in the bushes, naked and fearful, because you cannot face God. And the problem is not God. The problem is not existence. The problem is separate existence. The problem is sin.

And all sin is based on original sin, the effects of which will be with us till death.

But again, let me be practical. When you fall into this existential dread, what are you to do?

The answer I have already given: nothing. Let the process take place. Wait trustingly for the advent of grace which will liberate you and give you joy. No efforts on your part will get you out of this anguish. Only God can help you; and his merciful love will be poured into your heart through the blood of Jesus, who is your Saviour and Redeemer.

But remember what I said earlier about the holistic dimension of religious experience. Take all possible remedies. Watch your diet. Take exercise. Follow the doctor's instructions. If you feel that you need therapy, talk to a counsellor. For the fact is that while this is a purification of the existential dimension of the collective unconscious, it is

also true that problems of your personal unconscious will
continue to surface. And you must take care of them.

Indeed, this dreadful state may look like clinical depression. Your comforters, like those of Job, may tell you this
– and they may not be totally wrong. For your state may
be accompanied by traces of depression stemming from
childhood problems; and your symptoms may closely
resemble those of a depressed person. Nevertheless, existential dread is not clinical depression. You are not sick.
You are facing reality. And faced with reality the naked
human is very, very vulnerable. He or she hides fearfully
in the bushes. Spirit and psyche recoil, filled with anguish
and darkness. Yet this darkness is great wisdom and you
are highly favoured by God.

And so you must wait patiently for the coming of Jesus.
He will not sleep for ever in the boat. He will come walking
on the waters and calm the storm. But in what way will he
come?

As the problem is separation, so the answer is reconciliation, conversion, union. And we can look on this from two
aspects.

First, there is a sense in which no being in the universe
is, or can be, separated from God. For God is present in
all things, holding them in existence. He is the Being of all
things; and without his action they would fall into nothingness. Neither are we separate from one another nor from
the universe. All is one in God.

And you and I, Thomas, if we think we are separated,
isolated, autonomous existences, are in sad illusion. This is
the illusion of the separate ego, a consequence of original
sin.

Now to get rid of this illusion of separateness you need
an intellectual conversion or an enlightenment by which

you lose the illusory, separate ego and find your true self. Losing the sense of separateness you come to realize that you are one with God, one with the universe, one with all men and women. You lose the illusion of God "out there" or reality "out there". This intellectual conversion, as you will immediately see, is not a reconciliation but a recognition of reality as it is: existentially I am not separate. Be open to this experience of enlightenment, Thomas, and you will find that you are greatly liberated.

I have said that metaphysically no being in the universe is separate from God. And yet there is a sense in which we, human beings, can really isolate ourselves. While remaining one with God metaphysically or existentially we can separate ourselves from him by sin. And what a mind boggling mystery this is! This is the mystery of freedom, the mystery of iniquity – a mystery that lies at the heart of Judaeo-Christian religion. The man and the woman sinned and were expelled from paradise. And we, too, can run away from our Father's house. Hence we pray:

"Never permit me to separate myself from thee again."

We separate ourselves when we refuse to accept love, when we refuse to give love, when we refuse to forgive. We separate ourselves when we build barriers between ourselves and others. This is real separation; and in its final, definitive and permanent form it is hell.

Just as the answer to the illusion of existential separation is intellectual conversion, so the answer to sinful separation is religious conversion. This comes through the gift of God's grace to us. Thanks to the blood of his only Son we are reconciled with our Father and with the whole universe that he created. Religious conversion is to accept his love and to love in return, so that our being is transformed from being-in-isolation to being-in-love. The love of God will suddenly or gradually pour into your heart, and you will find that, like the prodigal, you are returning to your

Father's house, sitting down to enjoy the delicious morsels of the fatted calf. Now you will cry out with Paul: "Who shall separate us from the love of Christ?" And you will answer with Paul: "For I am sure that neither death . . . nor anything else in all creation, will be able to separate us from the love of God in Christ Jesus our Lord" (Romans 8:39). Now you are filled with joy, as the gnawing sense of separation and guilty fear which made you hide naked in the bushes is replaced by the relaxed sense of sin forgiven and of self united with God by Love.

At the right time Christ died for the ungodly, and the love of God was poured into our hearts by the Holy Spirit who was given to us. I have distinguished intellectual and religious conversion; but these two may come together in one joyful reconciliation, when your sorrow is turned into joy.

After passing through this tunnel of existential dread, Thomas, you will emerge into the light as a new man. You will find yourself in a world you never dreamt existed. This is a world of enlightenment, the world of the Spirit.

FIFTEEN

*

Night

I have said that the mystical life is a journey without maps.
No one can give a clear picture of what is happening, much
less of what will happen. And so some mystics are silent,
while others make use of symbols which are like a finger
pointing to the moon. Among these symbols one of the
most powerful and intriguing is that of night. As mysticism
is a journey without maps, so it is a journey into the night.

We all know that night can be a time of profound human
experience. Many artists, writers and thinkers sleep with
paper and pencil beside their bed in order to jot down the
inspirations that arise in their mind and heart at night.
Others, more modern, keep a tape-recorder close to their
head. They know that night is a time of great wisdom, of
great creativity, when powerful insights issue from the
unconscious, either in dreams or during the twilight zone
between sleeping and waking. And night is a time of
problem-solving and of growth. How often we go to sleep
with a problem and waken to find it solved!

Night is, too, a time of religious experience. We know
that Jesus spent nights in prayer, as did many great
religious men and women. Think of Paul. You remember
his vision in the night, of a man begging him to come to
Macedonia. And remember how, on his journey to Rome,
he spoke of the angel that appeared to him at night, assuring
him that he must appear before Caesar.

Dreams are of great significance throughout the Bible.

115

As the Spirit acts in our hearts during the day, so also he acts in dreams at night. But in both cases discernment is very necessary. Do not take dreams at their face value, but distinguish between good spirits, evil spirits and your own little ego. I myself believe that even when we do not dream or recall our dreams, religious experience continues. If you live a life of constant prayer, particularly of contemplative prayer, then this prayer will continue during sleep; and growth will take place, as it did in that man who planted seed and went to sleep, and, lo and behold, the seed grew he knew not how. In the same way, during sleep the Spirit is mysteriously at work in the most secret parts of your heart.

Night can be a time of terror. Nurses will tell you of the panic that descends on patients during the night. They are close to the unconscious, with its frightening contents. Mystics, too, have feared the night. During the day they were at peace but at night the darkness seemed to enter into their very souls, leaving them anguished, trembling and helpless. It was at night that they frequently wrestled with the devil – and, more often, with the demons of their own unconscious. But this painful struggle was purifying and purgative, tearing out the very roots of sinfulness lodged in the subliminal areas of the mind.

Night is a time when one does not see. One is groping in the dark. One is in unknowing and uncertainty. And it is frightening not to know where one is going or what strange being will pop up from we know not where.

Night is a time of love. Tender is the night. It is a time of romance. It is a time of the silver moon and the twinkling stars. It is a time of intimacy and profound communion. It is the time when bride and bridegroom are united in loving embrace. Tender is the night. Such nights are more lovely than the dawn and are filled with joy. For the bride is guided by love alone. She has no other light than that which burns in her heart. Warm and tender is the night.

As day is the *yang* so night is the *yin*. As day is the sun, so night is the moon. It is the dark, the feminine, the silent, the mystical, the profound, the unitive, the *yin*.

For all these reasons night is a powerful symbol. It symbolizes a mystical prayer that has no images, no concepts, no reasoning and thinking – a prayer of unknowing. It symbolizes a state of consciousness that is burdensome, heavy, painful, fearful, depressing. It depicts a prayer that is filled with love, union, ecstasy, delight. It symbolizes a time of wisdom, enlightenment and creativity. Night, like mystical prayer, is paradoxically full of joy and full of fear.

But let me now look at night in traditional mystical theology.

For Saint John of the Cross night is dynamic. The dark night is an inflow of God into the soul or it is, in the extraordinary and paradoxical words of Dionysius, a ray of darkness which strikes and pierces the soul, leaving her wounded, hurt and moaning. It is precisely the intensity of the divine light that blinds the soul and plunges her into painful darkness, just as the light of the sun blinds the bat and as the excessive light on the road to Damascus blinded Paul, leaving him groping and perplexed in the darkness.

Nor is this mere theory. When you enter this contemplative path, Thomas, there will be times, it is true, when the dark night is like a huge static, black curtain before which you sit in silent helplessness. But there will be other times when the darkness assails you like the Dionysian ray, and you cry out in pain. For the darkness seems to pour into your heart, breaking it into pieces.

And yet this is a time of exquisite wisdom. The dark

night, I repeat, is an inflow of God into your mind and heart. It is a secret or mystical wisdom that surpasses anything the human faculties (memory, understanding and will) are capable of grasping. It is a wisdom that human consciousness can never contain nor understand. It is a light the human person cannot endure. Yes, yes. Humankind cannot bear too much reality.

Saint John of the Cross speaks of three nights: the night of the senses, the night of the spirit, the night of God. He divides the nights in this way because he is a scholastic theologian who sees the human person as body, soul, and spirit. But he is aware that in practice these three nights are not neatly divided. They overlap and intermingle in such wise that the senses continue to be purified in the night of the spirit and the spirit purified in the night of the senses; and the night of God dominates all.

In **the night of sense** one is left without affective consolation. This is night only in a transferred meaning of the word. It is the time when one is well nigh overwhelmed by the fears and anxieties and lusts of the unconscious, about which I have already spoken.

The second night is **the night of the spirit**, also called the night of faith. Here it is necessary to distinguish between faith and belief, recalling that faith is the knowledge that comes from religious love, the knowledge that comes from total commitment. It is the knowledge or, better, the wisdom of one whose being is becoming being-in-love. But such wisdom is supra-conceptual and dark. One does not see. And so, paradoxically, the night of faith could be called the night of doubt. In the dark night one seems to doubt everything; but now one's faith commitment is strongest. One believes not because one has seen or heard or experienced; one believes because one believes. "Blessed are those who have not seen and yet believed" (John 20:29).

And then **God is like night**. It is not that God is darkness in himself. Far from it. He is inaccessible light. But he is like night to us because of the weakness of our human faculties. In other words, we must distinguish between God and the human experience of God. Let me put it like this:

> God is *light* in himself, but *darkness* to us
> God is *all* in himself, but *nothing* to us
> God is *fullness* in himself, but *void* to us

It follows that the night, the darkness, the nothingness, the void are the highest wisdom. Let me explain why this wisdom causes great suffering.

As I have said, the human faculties, incapable of facing up to the infinite light of God, cry out in agony and pain. And the weakness, imperfection and sinfulness of the human person greatly enhance this suffering. It is like a sodden log of wood plunged into the fire, which, precisely because of its dampness, gives off ugly black smoke for a while. But eventually, as the dampness is removed, the log burns brightly and is even transformed into the fire. It becomes the fire. In the same way the soul is "divinized" through the agonizing fire of love.

It is important to remember, Thomas, that the nights are transitional, leading to the time when the log and the fire are one. During this painful time you must learn the art of non-action, as I have already said. You must learn also to accept yourself.

For in these turbulent times you become very vulnerable. In their dark nights wise and holy contemplative people have done strange things. They have fallen in love with some unlikely person like the bishop who fell for the red-haired actress. Or they have turned to alcohol or some kind of addiction, or they have succeeded in making themselves a laughing stock before the world. But this has been a salutary experience; and so it will be with you. If anything like this happens, pick yourself up and keep going, with a smile and a song.

But let me return to the purgation that is taking place in your mind and heart and spirit.

God is purifying you in order that he may work through you and act, not in your way but in his own very mysterious way. If you are open to the loss of your ego and all the pain that this entails, you may find yourself resonating with the extraordinary words of Jesus; "Truly, truly, I say to you, he who believes in me will also do the works that I do; and greater works than these will he do, because I go to the Father" (John 14:12). You will do great, great things; and this will be the action not of your little ego but of Jesus himself, who having gone to the Father has returned in the Holy Spirit. He will be in you and will act through you: not through your little ego but through your big, universal self. "It is no longer I who live, but Christ who lives in me" (Galatians 2:20).

And so the dark night is the royal road to God. It is not the esoteric road of a few privileged mystics: it is the road of every human being who approaches a God of inaccessible light or darkness. One who would go to God must be purified from sin (and here again we are back with the Genesis story and the state of fallen nature), though purification differs with different people. It differs in intensity, since some are called to the heights and others to lower peaks; and it differs in duration for the same reason: star differs from star in glory.

But in all cases the final enlightenment is the beatific vision wherein one sees God face to face. Now the light which formerly plunged the poor soul into darkness and made her cry out with pain renders her ecstatically happy. In this life, to see God face to face through faith brings frightful suffering: in eternity, to see God face to face brings indescribable joy. Those who are not fully purified in this life (says the traditional mystical theology) must pass through the dark night in purgatory, since there is an inexorable law that one who goes to God must be purified. But even after this purification the unaided soul cannot look on the face of God. Her faculties need special assistance called the light of glory (the *lumen gloriae*) to enable her to face God and not die.

I have said that the night of some is longer and more intense than that of others, since some people need more purification than others. But now let me add that there is a third class of men and women who pass through deep purificatory suffering not for themselves but for the world in which they live. Such people are chosen to be with Jesus in Gethsemane. With Paul they say: "Now I rejoice in my sufferings for your sake, and in my flesh I complete what is lacking in Christ's afflictions for the sake of his body, that is, the church" (Colossians 1:24).

Night is a time of sleep. And what a beautiful gift this is! Sleep, gentle sleep, nature's soft nurse. In the mystical life some people go through cruel periods of insomnia and terror. How long and oppressive is the night! It is as though they hear the frightening words: "Sleep no more, Macbeth . . . sleep no more!" And then they realize the beauty of sleep that steeps their senses in forgetfulness. And when it is all over they thank God for the gift of sleep, chief nourisher in life's great feast. O night more lovely than the dawn!

SIXTEEN

---*---

Prayer of Suffering

I have spoken about a prayer of just being, and I have said that this is a prayer of being in love. Closely allied to this, Thomas, is a prayer of just suffering. When suffering comes to you (and sooner or later it comes to everyone) don't look or search for any special method of prayer. Just be. Just sit and accept your cross; accept it totally into the depths of your being. How easily I say this but how terribly anguishing is this prayer – and how terribly powerful! Remember that you need no words or thoughts. This prayer is a silent acceptance of the suffering of your life. That suffering may be sickness or rejection or separation from a loved one, or loneliness or failure or loss of reputation or misunderstanding or fear of death. Or it may be existential dread: the suffering of separated being. Whatever it is, sit with it. Don't run away. Don't try to escape. Don't fight. Sit with your cross.

I here mention the suffering of your personal life. But just as you have a personal unconscious and a collective unconscious, so your suffering may arise from your personal life or from the life of the whole human family. When your prayer matures and you come to the night of the spirit you will find that your cross is the suffering of the world. Then the cries of the hungry, the anguish of the oppressed, the agony of the tortured, the depression of those suffering from AIDS, the despair of those contemplating suicide, the darkness of those without faith – all this will be your cross, as it was the cross of one who sweated blood in Gethsemane.

In order to pray in this way you must first see your cross. Alas, there is a human tendency to pretend that suffering does not exist, to refuse to face reality, to push it into the unconscious, where it festers and causes all kinds of problems. And here Buddhism has something to teach us. As you know, Buddhism is based on the Four Noble Truths, the first of which is the truth of universal suffering and runs as follows:

Life is suffering

or

Existence is suffering

or

All is suffering

"How terrible!" exclaimed some wise Westerners. "How life-denying!" But modern psychology begins to refute them, saying that a grasp of this principle is pretty healthy: it is a healthy thing to realize once and for all that life is not easy, that life is full of suffering. Psychologists even begin to talk about the advantages of failure in business or in human relations, saying that such failure can promote human growth and maturity.

And as suffering is at the heart of Buddhism so the cross is at the heart of Christianity, as Paul knew well when he said that he wanted to know nothing except Jesus and him crucified. And so, Thomas, I tell you again: face the suffering of life; look at it; accept it. The one who does not take up his cross cannot be the disciple of Jesus. Above all, face the cross in prayer. When you are called to this prayer

of just suffering, don't escape into pious and holy consid-
erations of any kind. Take up your cross and be.

And as you practise this prayer of suffering, as you silently
open your heart to the cross, you will find something very,
very, precious. You will find that there is no quicker road
to enlightenment than this. You will find, as Paul found,
that in the cross is consummate wisdom. There is no better
school than that of suffering.

How well Shakespeare put it when he said: "Sweet are
the uses of adversity which, like the toad, ugly and
venomous, wears yet a precious jewel in his head." Yes, in
the midst of ugly adversity – whether it be rejection or
sickness or abandonment or failure – is a precious jewel.
Happy are you when you find this jewel and rejoice in its
sparkling beauty. Then you will appreciate existentially
the words of Jesus that his yoke is sweet and his burden is
light. From within the prayer of suffering will arise deep
peace and joy that the world cannot give and that no one
can take from you. This is indeed a jewel, a pearl of great
price.

And so I urge you, when the time comes, to make this
great prayer of suffering. Just sit and accept your cross.
Let the pain come. Accept it. As with existential prayer,
you may be tempted to think that you are wasting your
time and that you would be better to get to work and do
something worthwhile. But don't give way to such a
temptation. For the fact is that there is no greater power in
the world than suffering. Suffering is where the action is –
if you will permit me to talk more paradox. Shakespeare
was brilliantly insightful when he saw the jewel in the head
of the toad: the sparkling jewel in the midst of adversity.

*

Suffering can be creative. If your prayer is one of suffering – just acceptance of suffering – you will find that your creativity is wonderfully actuated. In the Bible one model of suffering is the woman in travail. Jesus himself uses this metaphor in his last discourse. The woman in childbirth writhes in pain, and then is filled with joy that a child is born into the world. In the same way, the disciples now suffer but their sorrow will be turned into joy when they give birth to their "child".

All this is saying that suffering is creative. It creates the child of art or music or poetry or drama or whatever (for nothing really great is achieved without suffering), but the prayer of suffering creates something even more significant.

Through the prayer of suffering your true self will be born. And this is enlightenment with a vengeance. You throw away your mask; you are knocked off your pedestal; your true character appears; your hidden potential rises up; your personality flowers in a new way; ineffable wisdom comes to possess your being. Above all, you discover a new capacity for love, for a universal love that goes on and on and on. And this is because you have lost your little ego and allowed your true self to be born – the true self that exists in God. And God is love.

The child born to the disciples was the kingdom of God. Primarily it was the kingdom within, a great interior enlightenment that came to birth in their hearts and overflowed into the whole world as they preached the Gospel to every creature and proclaimed that Jesus Christ is Lord. This initial enlightenment about the kingdom ripened in a supreme enlightenment wherein they shed their blood to witness again to all the nations that Jesus Christ is Lord.

*

I have said that the suffering of contemplation gives birth to enlightenment. Now let me add that this enlightenment is a great liberation, liberating us from the addictions that formerly tortured us, whether in the conscious or unconscious mind. I mean not only addiction to alcohol or tobacco or drugs or chemicals or chocolate or whatever, but also to human relationships. Yes, Thomas, we sometimes think we love another person when in fact our love is addictive, dependent drug-love. We need to be freed from such compulsive love of the little ego, to find the expanding *agape* of the true self. And then we can love authentically.

Again, this enlightenment liberates us from addiction to religious experience. For, Thomas, we can get addicted to certain prayers and pious practices; we can mistake the gifts of God for God himself. We can get addicted to sitting in the lotus, to searching for enlightenment, to enjoying consolation; and the mystics give stern warnings about addiction to visions and voices and revelations and all such things. It is a great liberation when we can let go. It is a great liberation when we can let go of the little self-centred ego to find the true self in God.

I have already referred to the Buddhist principle that all is suffering. Now let me pass on to a mind-boggling paradox. The Heart Sutra, a pillar of Buddhist practice and a constant source of inspiration for Zen meditators, makes the astounding assertion that *there is no suffering*. This is quite shocking; and it is meant to be shocking. It is meant to shock you into the realization that when one finds one's true self, totally liberated from desire and fear, suffering is no longer suffering. It runs parallel to the statement of Jesus that his yoke is sweet and his burden light.

And in the Christian path suffering has brought such profound enlightenment and such overwhelming joy that holy men and women have never wanted to be without it. Like Paul they have said: "But far be it from me to glory except in the cross of Our Lord Jesus Christ . . ." (Galatians 6:14). Like Paul they have rejoiced in their sufferings. Like Paul they have loved the crucified and the cross to which he was nailed. When you come to the enlightenment that suffering is your friend, then life on earth is paradise.

Some years ago I visited the castle of the family of Saint Francis Xavier in Javier in Spain. There in the family chapel I saw a thirteenth-century crucifix of "the smiling Christ". It is an ordinary crucifix showing a Jesus in great pain. But on his lips is the flicker of a smile.

In recent times we have come to see the power of suffering to effect social change. When men and women are willing to go to prison, to suffer and to die for their convictions, then things begin to happen. The power of suffering was impressed upon the whole world by Mahatma Gandhi. But in recent times we have seen it shine with even great lustre in the so-called People Power of the Philippines. What a shock, what a salutary shock, the world received on seeing helpless and defenceless men and women standing resolutely before tanks and guns! It was as though they said: "Kill us if you wish. We'll suffer. We'll die." And willingness to suffer and die proved infinitely more powerful than willingness to kill and maim and destroy. Those among us who thought that money and might were all-powerful got a rude awakening.

Yet does not Paul speak of the power of weakness? "When I am weak then I am strong" (2 Corinthians 12:10). Paul glories in his infirmity. And the Philippine people also were most strong when they were weak. What a lesson for the world!

*

But let me turn to a significant passage in the gospel. You remember how Jesus spoke about his coming passion and death, and Peter, out of the goodness of his big heart, remonstrated with the Lord saying: "God forbid, Lord! This shall never happen to you." And Jesus turned and said, "Get behind me, Satan! You are a hindrance to me; for you are not on the side of God, but of men" (Matthew 16:23).

What a shock poor Peter got! But he was meant to get a shock. Here Jesus is the Zen Master who knows that only a severe shock or jolt will bring Peter to enlightenment about the value of suffering. Jesus loves Peter (and Peter is well aware of this) and has no intention of hurting his feelings. He knows that philosophical or common-sensical argument will not bring Peter to enlightenment. Only a severe shock will bring about the necessary conversion.

And this passage is interesting from yet another viewpoint. It shows a very vulnerable Jesus. The words of Peter, his best friend, are a temptation, a continuation of the Satanic temptations in the wilderness. Jesus also feared suffering; he could be tempted to avoid his cross. What a mystery is here!

I have spoken to you about the prayer of suffering. Millions of people throughout the world are practising this prayer. Some may not know they are praying. Some may not even explicitly believe in God. But their suffering is saving the world and they are united with one who died crying: "*Lama Sabacthani!*"

SEVENTEEN

*

Being-in-Love

No need to say, Thomas, that Christian contemplation is a path of love. It is nothing other than total fidelity to the greatest of all commandments, to love God with one's whole heart and soul and mind and strength, and one's neighbour as one's self. Put this into practice and you will go far on the road of mystical contemplation.

However, let me immediately add that you cannot by your own efforts keep this greatest of all commandments. You cannot love totally without the prior gift of God's love for you. The old authors keep stressing that in all prayer the initiative comes from God. Christian contemplation, they remind us, is the response to a gift. "We love, because He first loved us" (1 John 4:19). So open your heart to receive the gift, which will surely be given, and then allow God's love to arise in your heart.

As you know, Bernard Lonergan speaks of religious conversion as a conversion to unrestricted and unconditional love. He is speaking about the human capacity for self-transcendence, and he goes on:

> That capacity becomes an actuality when one falls in love. Then one's being becomes being-in-love. Such being-in-love has its antecedents, its causes, its conditions, its occasions. But once it has blossomed forth and as long as it lasts, it takes over. It

is the first principle. From it flow one's desires and
fears, one's joys and sorrows, one's discernment of
values, one's decisions and deeds.

(Method in Theology, p. 105)

From this one can conclude that being in the fullest and
richest sense of the word is being-in-love. As you walk in
the mystical path your being is, oh, so gradually, becoming being-in-love. This is a slow process of conversion and
enlightenment. Born in the state of being-in-isolation we
gradually become being-in-love. Yet there is always the
danger of falling back into isolation, such is the weakness
of our human nature; and it is always possible to separate
ourselves from the totality. Moreover, our being-in-love
is always partial; we are always on the way, always
becoming. God alone is totally being-in-love; and we
reach fullness not as separate entities but in Him. And
so we can say:

Being = Being-in-love
Being-in-love = Being-in-God

And Lonergan's description of the man or woman who has
fallen hopelessly in love recalls the Song of Songs and the
living flame of love and the blind stirring of love. Here love
has become a raging fire at the core of one's being: from it
flows everything else. Lonergan continues:

Being in love with God, as experienced, is being in
love in an unrestricted fashion. All love is self-
surrender, but being in love with God is being in
love without limits or qualifications or conditions
or reservations. Just as unrestricted questioning is
our capacity for self-transcendence, so being in love
in an unrestricted fashion is the proper fulfilment
of that capacity.

(Ibid, pp. 105, 106)

All this, I maintain, is a good description of contemplative
prayer, which is existential living in love that goes on and

on and on, love which never ends because it is directed to the Infinite God.

This love is first experienced as a great awakening. The old mystical authors quoted (or misquoted) the Song of Songs – "Do not awaken love before its time." They meant that as there is a time for everything under the sun, so there is a time for the awakening of love. Wait for that time. Don't rush into mystical prayer. Don't think you can awaken it by techniques of breathing or mantra-reciting or anything else. However valuable these may be, they will not of themselves awaken love. Another will awaken love in your heart. At first his call may be frightening; but later you will dance for joy.

And once awakened, this love will lead you to one-pointedness. It will carry you beyond reasoning and think-ing, beyond imagining and conceptualizing, into the myst-ical silence, into the cloud of unknowing, into the blessed night. It will open up those subliminal areas of the psyche in which dwell sublime wisdom and dynamic power.

But let me look at some further consequences of this awakening of love.

Love leads to emptiness. It leads to a condition like that of one who emptied himself taking the form of a slave, who emptied himself when he knelt to wash the feet of his disciples, who experienced a total emptiness when he cried out, *Lama Sabacthani*. And he told his disciples, as he tells you and me, to love one another as he had loved them. That is why we can contemplate the emptiness of a Paul who suffered the loss of all things and of a Saint John of the Cross with his *nada, nada, nada*.

And so, Thomas, if you walk the path of love you will find that you are emptied, that you become nothing. But out of this emptiness and nothingness will emerge a great plenitude like that of one to whom God gave a name that is above all names, a name before which every knee will bow and every tongue confess that Jesus Christ is Lord, to the glory of God the Father.

For as love leads to emptiness so, too, it leads to self-transcendence and to ecstasy. In this book I have constantly spoken about losing the little ego and finding the big self. I have also said – and now I say it again – that you must not stop at this big self. You must transcend it in order to fall into God. And the only way (yes, the only way) to transcend the big self is to love.

Nothing is more important in the Christian life than self-transcendence, and there are three degrees within it.

I transcend myself **cognitionally** when I make an objective judgement stating that such-and-such is true and always will be true, even if I, a contingent being, never existed. In affirming that "Being is" I go beyond myself, leaving my little ego behind; I transcend myself in an intellectual conversion. If you can say with joyful objectivity and conviction that *being is*, then, moving out of a habitat and entering a universe, you are philosophically enlightened.

You transcend yourself **ethically**, when you make a judgement of value, saying that such and such conduct is good, apart from the satisfaction or advantage it gives to you. Now you are in the realm of self-forgetfulness and moral objectivity. When you follow the dictates of conscience to the point of losing everything, as did Thomas More, you are ethically enlightened.

And you transcend yourself **religiously** when you fall in love with God in response to his love for you. When the author of *The Cloud* speaks of total self-forgetfulness (self is buried beneath a cloud of forgetting), and when he speaks about destroying the knowing and feeling of one's being, he is talking about nothing less than the ecstasy of self-transcendence. Through love one comes to live in the person one loves and forgets not only one's little ego but even the big self.

Love leads to authenticity. When you are in love with God in an unrestricted way you are on the path to becoming authentically human. In the past those of us who studied Aristotle learned that every rational animal was a human being, whether that rational animal was a babe or a grandmother, a crook or a saint. But in modern culture we begin to see that one can be human authentically or inauthentically; and to become authentically human one must love in a total way. Consequently, the mystics, far from being oddballs (though they had their oddities and quirks like everyone else) were pre-eminently authentic human beings.

Love leads to a conversion that is nothing less than a revolution in consciousness. Such is the Christian mystical path upon which you have embarked. Let me repeat it: you and I were born in the state of fallen nature, and the mystical path leads to the state of holiness and integrity in which one loves God totally. We are born as being-in-isolation and we become being-in-love. This is Christian conversion. This is Christian enlightenment.

In the brief passages I have quoted, Lonergan speaks of being in love without restriction; but elsewhere he describes the same phenomenon in terms of total commitment. It is by being totally committed that I walk the road of individuation; it is by being totally committed that I go beyond myself to God.

*

But what is the nature of this love?

Let me say that while there are two commandments – to love God and to love one's neighbour – these two are so closely intertwined that we can call them one. So always keep in mind that the love which floods your heart in silent meditation is the same love that goes out to every person you meet. It is like the love of our Father who makes his sun rise on the evil and on the good, and sends his rain on the just and the unjust. As you grow in contemplative prayer, you will find that, as you walk down the street or stand on the train, your heart goes out in love and compassion to everyone you see. I am reminded of that beautiful passage in the Second Vatican Council which tells us to make ourselves the neighbour of all men and women, actively helping them when they cross our path, whether we meet an old person abandoned by all, a foreign labourer unjustly looked down upon, a refugee, a child born of an unlawful union and wrongly suffering for a sin he or she did not commit, or a hungry person who disturbs our conscience by recalling the voice of the Lord: "As long as you did it for one of these, the least of my brothers, you did it for me" (Matthew 25:40).

Through contemplation you become a fountain that pours forth loving waters in all directions. Anyone who comes within the radius of that fountain – old or young, rich or poor, man or woman, saint or sinner, friend or enemy – gets splashed by love. Such is the universal love of *agape*. Through it human beings become perfect as their heavenly Father is perfect.

And yet *agape* can also be very passionate. The passionate love of God is indeed a central theme of the Hebrew scriptures; and when the mystics come to describe their experience they often turn to the bride-bridegroom theme in the Song of Songs. I urge you to read this exquisite love poem again and again, and to resonate with its music and its symbolism. Here I cannot discuss its myriad interpretations; but I would like to comment briefly on a passage that may help you in your journey.

A central theme of the whole poem is the awakening of love. Recall that passage where the bride is asleep but her heart is awake: "I slept but my heart was awake." And then comes the knocking at the door:

"Hark! My beloved is knocking."

The knocking at the door is an archetypal symbol found throughout the Hebrew scriptures as well as in Revelation, where Jesus stands at the door and knocks. It is also found in that terrible Shakespearian scene where Macbeth, after murdering the innocent king, hears the knocking on the door and trembles.

In human life Jesus knocks on the door. This is the awakening of love. For Jesus is the tremendous lover who knocks and calls. We either open the door and invite him in; or we follow him out into the night. We must not, and cannot, ignore him.

Many contemplatives resonate with this powerful symbolism. Vividly they hear the knocking on the door. Perhaps in a dream they hear the footsteps on the veranda and the knock, knock, knock. Or they may dream of an intruder banging on the door and trying violently to break in. Or (yet another symbol) they may hear a bell that awakens and calls them. Or they may hear their name called at night: "Samuel! Samuel!"

And the knocking on the door or the sound of the bell is frightening. For we don't want to be woken up: we prefer to sleep. We are terrified of the unknown, afraid of the dark. In the same way the bride trembles with fear; she does not want to get out of bed. "I had put off my garment, how could I put it on? I had bathed my feet, how could I soil them?" (Song of Songs 5:3). But the lover is persistent: he puts his hand on the latch. And then what pathos! She tells us:

> "I opened to my beloved,
>   but my beloved had turned and gone."

Out she goes into the night in search of the one she loves. She is sick with love. She is wounded and beaten by the watchmen. But on and on she goes until she finds him whom she loves.

What a journey into the night! But the commentary of Saint John of the Cross is like a cold shower in its blunt realism:

> Whoever refuses to go out at night in search of the Beloved and to direct and mortify his will, but rather seeks the Beloved in his own bed and comfort as did the bride (Ct 3:1) will not succeed in finding him; as this soul declares who found him when it departed with longings of love.

And so, Thomas, when the call of love comes, get out of bed! Leave the security of warm blankets and refreshing sleep. Go out into the night after Jesus. But let me tell you a secret. Even if you do refuse to get up, even if from human weakness you stay under those warm and cosy blankets, this lover will not take a refusal. He will continue to knock, to ring the bell, to torment you until you get up and follow him.

Now I need hardly say that this knocking at the door symbolizes the crisis about which I wrote in an earlier chapter. It is frightening because no one wants to get out of bed, out of her room, and follow Jesus into the night of unknowing. "Where am I going?" she asks. "Is this knock a call of death? And if so, what is the nature of that death? Is it physical death or is it the death of all that I have known and loved until now? Who is this Jesus who is knocking? Is death knocking at my door?"

Such is the awakening of love. Such is the call to enlightenment. When you follow Jesus out into the night you are moving towards that conversion wherein your being becomes being-in-love. If you seek, you will find. And what a union that is! Listen to Saint John of the Cross:

Upon my flowering breast, kept wholly for himself alone,
There he stayed sleeping, and I caressed him.

Here is the ecstasy of mystical love.

The bride-bridegroom story leads to another question that greatly preoccupies modern people. How does the being-in-love theme relate to the love of friendship and intimacy? I have spoken of the *agape* which radiates upon everyone who comes your way. But does this *agape* play a role in intimate love between man and woman, or in intimate love between persons of the same sex?

The Second Vatican Council speaks eloquently about the role of *agape* in married life, saying that authentic married love is caught up into divine love; and it speaks beautifully of this "many-faceted love welling up . . . from the fountain of divine love". It is as though human love is divinized by divine love; or as though there was a marriage between *agape* and *eros*.

But human, loving intimacy is not restricted to marriage. Friendship and interpersonal relations are the core and centre of novels and movies, of drama and poetry in our day. It seems that modern people are longing for intimate union with another human being. But after Freud it became axiomatic that human intimacy demands genital, sexual expression.

Now, however, the Freudian era has come to an end and the sexual revolution is past history. Even as I write, a vast cultural change is taking place in the whole world, and we hear the question: Is it possible for people to love deeply and intimately while remaining chaste and even celibate? Can deep love and friendship between people of the same sex or of the opposite sex coexist with chastity and celibacy?

To this question the Christian tradition, including the tradition of the New Testament, answers with a resounding "Yes". Let us recall the great scene when Jesus asks Peter: "Do you love me more than these?" and Peter answers: "Yes, Lord, I love you." Was that love anything less than total commitment? Or, again, think of the beloved disciple and Mary Magdalene and Martha. Other examples of deep and chaste love between committed mystics fill the pages of history.

And so I urge you, Thomas, to open your heart to friendship and intimacy, remembering that your friendships are an extension of your contemplative prayer. They are indeed contemplative friendships. As mystical contemplation necessarily brings suffering and emptiness, dark nights and enlightenment, so too will intimate friendship bring suffering and emptiness, dark nights and enlightenment. As mystical contemplation leads to human authenticity so does mystical friendship; as mystical contemplation leads to self-transcendence so also does mystical friendship. You will find that deep purification takes place, and that you become transparent to another person and she to you, with a transparency that leads to an indwelling that Freudian psychology cannot comprehend.

Shakespeare knew something about human love, as he knew something about the Gospel. What enlightenment shines through his cry: "Let me not to the marriage of true minds admit impediment", and he goes on to say that love is not love which alters when it alteration finds. Again, love transcends time and transcends everything: "Love's not time's fool . . ." For love bears all things, believes all things, hopes all things, endures all things. Love never ends.

Love never ends. Saint John of the Cross says that the living flame of love burning in the heart of the mystic is the Holy Spirit. And you will find that as your love grows it is no longer your love but the love of another who dwells within. You will adapt Saint Paul and say: "It is no longer I who love but Christ loves in me."

EIGHTEEN

*

Dialogue

I have urged you, Thomas, to invite Buddhists and Hindus, Muslims and Jews to your centre, and to let them pray or meditate in accordance with their own convictions and beliefs. In this you will find an outstanding model in Pope John Paul, who in October 1986, with the inspiration of a prophet, invited the leaders of the world religions to pray and fast for peace at Assisi. Those who were present speak in moving terms of the humble demeanour of the Dalai Lama, the major Rabbi of Rome, the Archbishop of Canterbury, Mother Teresa and many others as they entered the small chapel where Saint Francis died on the bare ground. All prayed in silence for a short time before dispersing to twelve different locations in Assisi, where they prayed according to their own unique traditions. In this way the unity and diversity of the world religions shone forth clearly.

And so, throughout the town of Saint Francis, arose prayer and meditation inspired by the Vedas, the Sutras, the Koran, the Avesta, the Psalms and the Gospel, with incense, flowers, water, fire and peace-pipe. In five Catholic Churches in Assisi crowds prayed before the Blessed Sacrament, while throughout the world men and women interceded for peace on earth. "The challenge of peace transcends all religions", said John Paul. The word peace is central to the worship of all religions: *shalom*, *shanti*, *heian*, *salam*, *mir*, *eirene*, *pax*. And he went on to say that they had not "come here for an interreligious conference on peace, but rather to invite the world to realize that there exists another dimension of peace and another way to promote it."

And it is for us, Thomas, to prolong and deepen the spirit of Assisi. It is for us to seek prayerful communion with men and women of other faiths, and to join them in prayer for world peace. What a challenge! It seems so different from anything we have known until now. And yet it may not be so different. Those assembled at Assisi felt united with the poor and humble Saint Francis.

Needless to say, there is a direct line from Assisi back to the Second Vatican Council, where the assembled fathers, acutely aware of a world rapidly coming together, stressed the necessity of peace and harmony and of dialogue between the great religions. Their most telling comments on dialogue were in the Decree on Ecumenism, which treats of the relationship between Christians of various denominations. The principles there enunciated, however, are equally valid for the wider dialogue between men and women of different faiths. I urge you to read this document and assimilate its teaching.

The basis of dialogue, says the Council, is prayer and *metanoia* or change of heart. "There can be no ecumenism worthy of the name without a change of heart", said the fathers. And again: "This change of heart and holiness of life, along with public and private prayer . . . should be regarded as the soul of the whole ecumenical movement and can rightly be called spiritual ecumenism."

From this *metanoia* will flow a humility, a charity, an esteem for those with whom we dialogue, a liberation from the arrogant one-up-manship which says "holier than thou". The Council quotes Saint Paul: "I, therefore, the prisoner of the Lord, exhort you to walk in a manner worthy of the calling with which you were called, with all humility and meekness, with patience, bearing with one another in love, careful to preserve the unity of the Spirit in the bond of peace" (Ephesians 4:1–3).

Again, the Council calls for self-examination, reminding Catholics that "their primary duty is to make an honest and careful appraisal of whatever needs to be renewed and achieved in the Catholic household itself . . ." It further insists on every effort to eliminate words and judgements that could be hurtful or unfair. It apologizes for injustices and sins against unity. And it makes a clarion call for profound study pursued with unflinching fidelity to truth.

All this inspires our dialogue with Buddhism. Remember that the first thing is a profound *metanoia* or change of heart whereby you commit yourself totally to Jesus and the Gospel. Never think that you must compromise on your Christian faith. Never think that you must temporarily prescind from your commitment to Christ in order to enter into the Buddhist experience. Such a stance is impossible – and authentic Buddhists do not expect it. Devote yourself totally to Jesus and the Gospel, and you will find (wonder of wonders) that as Paul was liberated from the law, so you are liberated from narrow sectarianism and bigoted legalism. You will find that your mind and heart are opened to the splendid riches of Buddhism and to the marvels that God has wrought through religions other than your own. For commitment to the Gospel opens your eyes to the good and holy wherever it may be.

Metanoia will lead you to humility – to a respect for Buddhist saints, Buddhist practices, Buddhist scriptures. Furthermore it will lead you to reform what is wrong within the Catholic household. Let me give you an example. While Catholics, according to the spirit of the Council, speak loudly and clearly about respect for human dignity and human rights throughout the world, there are certain elements within the Church which continue to trample on human dignity and to treat human beings as things. Surely this is an evil we must strive to reform. Here is an area in which we must ask humbly for conversion.

Be that as it may, you will find that this dialogue opens you to a whole new area of religious experience which our forebears did not know. The road to Damascus. The road to Assisi. The road to New Delhi and Tokyo and Beijing. The road to nowhere.

The good news of Vatican Two spread rapidly. In Japan, Christians were already learning from Zen; and now the interest grew, and it continues to grow today. Less well known is the flourishing dialogue in the Philippines: in Mindanao, Christians and Muslims join in prayer and in sharing contemplative experience.

From the West in 1968 came the wise man Thomas Merton, whose journey to Bangkok, tragic yet triumphant, created history. Merton described himself as a pilgrim, open to learn, and hoping that Asian monasticism would help the Christian West now floundering in tumultuous crisis. Most interesting was his visit to Dharmsala where he met the Dalai Lama. Humorously, almost cynically, Merton talked about the conversation in which the Tibetan leader asked about the vows – were they just a promise to stick around for life or did they represent a commitment to a mystical ascent? Merton stood for (and claimed that the Dalai Lama stood for) the mystical interpretation. More-over, he insisted that it was at this level that Eastern and Western monks could meet. Both, he maintained, were preoccupied with the radical inner depths of their religious beliefs; both were concerned with inner transformation and with moving towards a breakthrough to a transcendental dimension of life. It was precisely on this deep, mystical level that fruitful encounter was possible.

On this point, Thomas, I agree completely with Merton. The vows should lead to that perfect love which is the centre of Christian mysticism. So let's get away from the legalistic asking permission and washing of hands. Merton is asking Christian monks to break through to enlightenment (though he does not explicitly use this word), and to enter into the mystical life in order that Christians and Buddhists may meet at the core of their being.

Other Western monks have followed in the footsteps of Merton. Some have come to Japan from Germany to practise Zen; and Japanese monks have returned the compliment. American monks and nuns have gone to Dharmsala in the footsteps of Merton to meditate with Tibetan monks and to enter into dialogue with the Dalai Lama, a dialogue which promises to be one of the most exciting and fruitful events of the next century.

From all that has been said it will be clear that there are various kinds of dialogue between religions. There is ordinary conversation and exchange between believers. There are academic and scholarly meetings between professors and experts. Again, there is the practical dialogue between believers who are working on a common project. However, another form of dialogue is particularly interesting for us here, namely the contemplative dialogue wherein people share personal, religious experiences. This can be (as a colleague of mine puts it) a wordless dialogue: both parties enter into a deep silence and a deep communion.

Such sharing of contemplative experience, however, is built on an *inner dialogue* which is the most important of all. This is a dialogue in which I open my mind and heart to receive the teaching of other religions: to be challenged and to be changed. It can be agonizingly painful but extremely fruitful. In this dialogue I do not need to talk to anyone. I simply read and learn about the other religion (in our case, Buddhism), and open myself to the development of an inner process which continues even during sleep. Through it I become aware of the difference between my Christianity and the other religion; but I also come to see my Christian faith in a new light. My notion of God is modified. I come to read the Gospel with new eyes. Perhaps I even see Jesus in a new way. In short, this inner dialogue is an enriching way of prayer, of contemplative prayer. The encounter with another religion is taking place not "out there" but in the depths of my being.

And as this inner dialogue progresses one can turn to the outer dialogue with contemplative men and women of other faiths. Merton beautifully describes such dialogue as communication leading to communion. When we can meet others at the level of inner silence our communion is very deep.

The Second Vatican Council turned its eyes towards those things which human beings have in common. And it came to the very obvious conclusion that what we have in common is our human nature, what we have in common is our humanity.

The great religions come together when they look at the inner structure of the human person. Saint Paul divides the human person into body, soul and spirit. And a careful reading of the whole Bible reveals a similar anthropology. So, too, the Christian mystics speak of body and soul, and then of the centre of the soul or the sovereign point of the spirit or the *scintilla animae*.

Now these three levels can be found, I believe, in the religious experience of all the great religions. Each religion, of course, has its own terminology, a terminology modified according to the culture in which the religion lives. But the three levels will always be there. The true self in Buddhism corresponds to the level of spirit, as does the divine spark in Hinduism.

And so the specifically religious dimension of the human person is the area of spirit where men and women are in love without restriction, and where they enter the deepest levels of mystical contemplation. Whereas science can study the body and the psyche, it cannot study the spirit since it can here find no sensible data from which to argue. Spirit, then, is the transcendental dimension – it is transcultural and, in a sense, transreligious. When people meet at the level of spirit they need no words: they can communicate or, more correctly, commune in profound silence. It is here that the most authentic dialogue takes place.

However, when we come together in dialogue it is not enough to relish what we have in common: we must beware of mutual narcissism or self-satisfaction. Remember that Assisi was not dialogue for dialogue's sake, but common prayer for world peace. In future could not the scope of this dialogue be extended to include prayer for the preservation of the human person, for the preservation of human values, for the preservation of our world?

For it is a truism to say that at this point in history the human family is facing total destruction. One could speak of nuclear war, international terrorism, destruction of the environment, contempt for human dignity, systematic torture, a hopeless arms race and a long, long list of dehumanizing tendencies. And the basic problem is that we have lost the sense of human dignity.

Now what the great religions have in common is reverence for the human person, for human values and, above all, for the human spirit. What they have in common is love for truth, for justice and for peace. The ideal of the compassionate Bodhisattva, the righteous one in Judaism and the saint in Christianity, are very similar. And so the believer of the great religions, following along the road to Assisi, can collaborate to create a spirituality that will preserve the human person and the world in which he or she lives.

When Jew and Christian, Hindu and Buddhist, Muslim and agnostic come together for prayer, the world will listen. And God will listen too.

NINETEEN

*

Discernment

Human life is a process of growth and development, and today, more than ever before, we have become aware of the phenomenon of psychic growth. Now we know that men and women keep growing psychically through childhood and adolescence to midlife and old age. We know that midlife and old age offer wonderful opportunities for the flowering of the personality and the discovery of one's authentic self. We believe that death is the last stage in growth, leading to a life which goes on and on into Infinite Love.

Human growth is not like that of the acorn becoming an oak. We grow to maturity through free decisions and choices which make us to be what we are and what we will be. There are small decisions made quickly and spontaneously. There are big decisions which demand thought and time and prolonged prayer. It is through these decisions, both small and big, that we chose our path in life.

By small decisions I mean when to work and when to play, when to study and when to watch TV, when to eat and when to fast, when to sleep and when to watch, when to visit the sick and when to play the guitar, when to have fun with friends and when to go to the chapel and pray, whether to vote for this political party or for that, whether to walk in peace marches or to stay home and study economics. Many of these decisions are concerned with timing: there is a time for everything under the sun.

By big decisions I mean the taking of a new path or a

new direction in life. Big decisions may be made through the crisis I mentioned in an earlier chapter. Big decisions may concern vocation or commitment to community or whatever. Big decisions were made by Paul and by Pilate.

Through these decisions, Thomas, you either build up your illusory ego or discover your true self. We are all keenly aware that the decisions of powerful statesmen can affect the lives of millions: we sometimes forget that the person most affected is the statesman himself. By these decisions he can make or destroy himself. Often this becomes clear when he is brought to trial or when he is judged by history. Then people ask: When did he take the fatal step that led to his downfall?

This problem of decision-making looms large amongst Catholics today. Between Trent and Vatican Two great emphasis was placed on the external teaching of the Church and on its exterior laws. The ideal was to obey humbly and submit joyfully to the rules of the visible Church. But then came the shift to interiority, with its emphasis on the self and the inner world of personal responsibility. The great John Henry Newman spoke vigorously for conscience; and the Second Vatican Council stated clearly that conscience is the glory of the human person – and according to it will he or she be judged. So responsible Catholics today feel more and more the need to be in touch with the inner voice of conscience. They want to be guided by the inner light, while still respecting the exterior law.

And so arises the challenge of discerning what to do and what not to do, and how to make decisions. It is true, of course, that some people make no decisions at all. They drift along with the crowd; and their decisions are made by *Newsweek* or *The Times* of London or *The Japan Times*. In this way they escape the agonizing and often protracted process of searching for God's will, or doing it, and thus becoming their true and unique selves. I know you do not belong to that category, Thomas. But before speaking about Christian discernment, let me digress for a moment to say a word about Socrates.

You remember how Socrates spoke of his inner *daimon* which warned him against certain courses of action. While defending himself against his accusers he spoke of this divine or supernatural manifestation which began in early childhood – a sort of voice that came to him, which, when it came, always dissuaded him from what he was proposing to do, and never urged him on. This voice debarred him from entering public life. And so Socrates, blessed with a wonderful sense of humour and a radical indifference to public opinion, asked embarrassing questions as he kept searching for the truth. And, of course, he was forced to drink hemlock. For people do not like the person who is faithful to the inner light and refuses to drift with the crowd. Such people are frequently killed, as were the prophets.

Socrates' inner voice was no doubt a charismatic gift of discernment, which some people possess from childhood. We find something parallel in Joan of Arc. If you meet a Christian with such a gift, remember that grace transforms these charisms and never destroys them. They are beautiful gifts, even when they lead to the death of the one who possesses them. But let me return to my theme.

In making decisions, Thomas, the modern ideal is to be authentically human, and with this in mind I urge you to assimilate and make your own the transcendental precepts:

Be attentive
Be intelligent
Be reasonable
Be responsible
Be in love

The ideal is that these precepts come to live in your unconscious mind, influencing your whole life and your every decision. If your decisions and choices are intelligent, reasonable, responsible and loving you will undergo intellectual, ethical and religious conversion. You will transcend yourself and attain to true humanity. But, needless to say, this is a struggle. For human nature has a tendency to be inattentive, stupid, unreasonable, irresponsible and hateful. And so a titanic struggle goes on, not only in individuals but also in civilizations and cultures. When a significant number of people strive to be faithful to these precepts a culture develops and progresses; when a large majority reject these precepts it declines. And in this context I believe that modern Western culture is in decline today.

Be that as it may, these precepts express the basic thrust of the human psyche. That is why I urge you to follow the voice of attention, intelligence, reasonableness, responsibility and love. This may sound simple. And, indeed, in the state of original justice it may have been simple (though even there the man and the woman listened to the voice of the serpent), but in our fallen state it is much more complex. I have already said that the human psyche is multi-layered and contains all kinds of voices. There is, for example, the voice of the super-ego. If psychologists are right (and in this perhaps they are) some people spend their lives listening to, and obeying, the voice of their mother. And besides this maternal voice there may be voices of anxiety, fear, depression, frustration, anger, despair – all that Ignatius calls desolation. Sometimes your inner life may be a maelstrom. In all this you may ask despairingly: Where are the voices of intelligence, responsiblity and love?

The fact is that we poor, weak human beings need education and training. But above all we need the grace of God, and about this I will now speak.

Of the transcendental precepts, Thomas, the one I want to highlight for you is the last: **Be in love**. This love is the answer to a prior call of God and it means (as I have already said) that your being becomes being-in-love. And now your decision-making becomes more distinctively religious: you are choosing between good and evil, or you are choosing between a path that leads to good and a path that leads to evil. The New Testament tells us clearly that the key to such choice is love: "This is the commandment, as you have heard from the beginning, that you follow love" (2 John 1:6). And to the Ephesians Paul writes: "And walk in love, as Christ loved us and gave himself for us, a fragrant offering and sacrifice to God" (Ephesians 5:2). When love is the leading voice in your psyche you are a follower of Jesus Christ, totally committed to the Gospel.

Love calls down the Holy Spirit, who comes to dwell in you, to guide you, to direct you. I urge you to read again and again the Last Discourse in Saint John where Jesus speaks of the Paraclete and of the inner guidance and strength He gives. Together with this I recommend to you the simple prayer, "Come, Holy Spirit" or, if you find the Latin more mellifluous, "*Veni, Sancte Spiritus*". Some people like to repeat this tiny prayer again and again and again for days and weeks and months and years, until gradually their whole lives are lived in sensitive docility to the indwelling

Spirit. Those small decisions, then, are made spontaneously under his gentle inspiration. For the Holy Spirit
comes to manifest himself at the core of one's being as a
living flame of love, a blind stirring of love, an obscure
sense of presence, a naked intent of the will. This is indeed
mysticism in action, since the lives of such people are
dedicated to doing God's will as revealed by the indwelling
Spirit.

Needless to say, no one is totally faithful to the Holy
Spirit for twenty-four hours each day. Saint Ignatius,
who is a master of discernment, presupposes that we will
make mistakes. Common-sensically he tells us to look
back, see the serpent's tail, and then make sure that the
same mistake is not repeated. As for the maelstrom, he
tells us to wait it out; to make no decision until the storm
has passed and we are capable of peacefully discerning the
voice of love. It seems to me that a distinctive feature of
Ignatian discernment is its extraordinary awareness of the
inner movements of the psyche. In this it resembles much
modern psychology, particularly that of people like Carl
Rogers.

If you do as I say, you will gradually come to realize that
discerning the Spirit is a gift. Sometimes it is like a sixth
sense. Holy men and women will sniff the air and say:
"Yes, the Spirit of God is here", or, "No, no. This is not
it". This is because the indwelling Spirit is sensitive to
good and evil wherever it may be. And let me add that
Jesus was acutely sensitive to the presence of good and evil.
At one time he rejoiced in the Spirit and cried: "I thank
thee, Father . . ." (Luke 10:21); and at another time he was
deeply troubled in Spirit and said: "Truly, truly, I say to
you, one of you will betray me" (John 13:31).

*

From what has been said it will be clear that when one
enters into mystical contemplation discernment takes on a
mystical character. Just as in mystical contemplation you
must let go of reasoning and thinking and discursive prayer,
so in mystical discernment you must let go of reasoning
and thinking and discursive reflection in order to live by
faith. Reasoning which was formerly your friend is now
your enemy. Saint John of the Cross expresses it characteristically by saying that you are safer when you walk in
darkness – without the light of reason. So let go of reason,
and attend to faith and wisdom and the movements of the
Spirit in the depth of your being. Above all, attend to the
blind stirring of love, to the living flame of love, to the
obscure but peaceful sense of presence, to the naked intent
of the will. For this inner movement will tell you what to
do and what not to do in the conduct of your daily life.
But, lest there be any misunderstanding, let me say a
further word about reason.

On the one hand, reasoning can be a snare and a trap. It
can smother the flame of love that is guiding you more
surely than the noonday sun. Again, I don't need to remind
you of the danger of rationalization: that people can spe-
ciously rationalize themselves into anything from nuclear
war to abortion. If only they could let go of reasoning and
attend to their deepest centre where God dwells, their
judgements would be so much more sure. On the other
hand, it is also true that you need reason *as a check*. When
you have felt the deep movement of the Spirit, when you
have heard the inner voice, when you have opened your
heart to the inspiration which is *yin*, you need the check of
reason which is *yang*. That is why I expressed some
reservation about the statement of Richard of St Victor
that when contemplation is born reason dies.

*

I said that Ignatius of Loyola was a master of discernment. Much of his prayer – and profoundly mystical that prayer was – was devoted to discerning what he should do and what he should not do. He learned by experience to listen to the Spirit. He was acutely aware of the existence of evil forces in the world, and he spoke constantly about the crafty enemy of our human nature. His discernment all began when he lay in bed, sick and wounded, and began to observe his own thoughts and feelings, asking himself where they led. After this he travelled all over Europe, from Rome to England and from Paris to Jerusalem, all the time attending to the inner movements, the mystical stir-rings that worked in the depth of his being. Let me quote to you one interesting example of his discernment process.

While in Manresa it often happened that on a bright day he could see something in the air near him. Because it was indeed very beautiful, it gave him great satisfaction. He could not discern very well what it was, but it looked like a serpent with many things that shone like eyes, though they were not eyes. He found great pleasure and consolation in seeing this thing, and the more he saw it the more his consolation grew. When it disappeared he became sad.

And so Ignatius found great consolation in the vision of the serpent. Yet at this time he was filled with scruples and fears and anxieties about the life he had undertaken. He even felt tempted to commit suicide. With great violence the temptation often came to him to throw himself into a large hole. But at first he made no connection between these temptations and the vision of the snake.

Then it happened that he was going to a church a little more than a mile from Manresa. The road ran next to the river Cardoner, and he sat down for a while with his face toward the river, which was running deep. While he was seated there, the eyes of his mind were opened; though he did not see any vision, he understood and had profound insight into a myriad of things relating to faith and theology; and this was such a powerful enlightenment that everything seemed new to him. He experienced a remarkable clarity in his understanding. He could later say that in the whole course of his life, through sixty-two years, even if he gathered up all the many graces he had received from God and all the many things he knew and added them together, he did not think they would amount to as much as he had received at that one time.

Such was the great enlightenment at the river Cardoner. After this had lasted for a time, he went to kneel before a nearby cross to give thanks to God. There the vision of the snake with many eyes appeared again. But while kneeling before the cross, he saw clearly that it did not have its usual beautiful colour; and with a strong affirmation of his will he knew very clearly that it came from the demon. For a long time after, it often appeared to him; but as a sign of contempt he drove it away with a staff he usually carried in his hand.

I have recounted the experience of Ignatius, more or less in his own words, but I like to interpret it in a Zen context. The vision of the serpent was *makyo*, which means the world of the devil; the imageless vision at the river Cardoner is the real *satori* or enlightenment. We know that at this time Ignatius was at a crossroads. Would he commit himself to a life of total fidelity to Jesus Christ and the Gospel? Or would he follow those romantic dreams of beautiful women? And it may be that this fascinating and seductive serpent was a projection of his unconscious, a projection of the part of his psyche that was calling him back. The experience at the Cardoner, on the other hand, was a core enlightenment, a real grasp of truth; and it enabled him to unmask the evil one, seeing the green-eyed monster as a subtle temptation.

Later he was to write picturesquely that the action of God in the Soul is like a drop of water falling gently into a sponge; and the action of evil forces is like rain pattering on a rock. This applies, I believe, to the above experience. The vision at the Cardoner, a core experience, was like the drop of water penetrating softly to the very centre of his being and bringing an immense awakening. The vision of the serpent, on the other hand, was somehow outside, like rain pattering on the rock; and it eventually lost its beauty, jolting him and depriving him of inner peace.

Ignatius wrote rules for discernment of spirits. But the whole Spiritual Exercises can be interpreted as a process of discernment. Confronted with weighty decisions or choices people frequently go through the Exercises in search of God's will.

The core of the Spiritual Exercises is total commitment to Jesus and to the Gospel. If you want to walk the path of love and goodness, says Ignatius, then follow Jesus in poverty and humiliation, and turn away from Satan, who invites you to riches and vanity and pride. And, of course, this is completely in conformity with the New Testament, where the supreme norm for discerning the spirit is Jesus himself – Jesus who has come in the flesh. Any spirit which leads you to cry out that Jesus is Lord comes from God: any spirit that leads you to say that Jesus is accursed comes from Satan. Such is the norm of John and Paul.

And a practical norm it is. Whatever leads you to Jesus in the flesh, Jesus in the eucharist, Jesus in the Gospel, Jesus in the poor and afflicted – whatever leads you to Jesus poor and humiliated is good. Use this norm, Thomas. If you find someone, for example, who is worried about her prayer, worried about her use of this method or that, ask the simple question: Does this lead you to Jesus in the flesh? If it does, it is good. If not, it is not for you.

Let me select from the Exercises some points that will be valuable for you.

Ignatius puts great stress on core commitment. If one's core commitment is for good, then whatever leads to good and is in conformity with this commitment will bring joy; and what leads to evil will bring disturbance. On the other hand, if one's core commitment is for evil, whatever leads to evil will bring joy, and whatever leads to good will bring disturbance. The vision of the serpent seemed at first to bring joy but, in fact, it brought disturbance and loss of peace. That is why Ignatius drove it away with his staff.

And so in this whole matter your core commitment is vital. Learn always to return to your centre and to renew your total commitment to Jesus and to the Gospel. About the art of returning to the centre I have learned much from Zen. Zen has taught me to get to my true self, to zero point, to the still point of the turning world. This is the point beyond subject and object where we can relish the timeless moment in total liberation from the inner drives and attachments and anxieties that cloud our judgement and make decisions difficult. This is the point at which one discovers Ignatian indifference to health rather than sickness, a long life rather than a short life, riches rather than poverty. If you can find this still point you will find great facility in discernment and in making your core commitment to Jesus and the Gospel.

*

Ignatius speaks of "consolation without previous cause", and he maintains that it belongs to God alone to give such consolation. If there is no apparent cause then (if one believes in Aristotle's principle of causality, as Ignatius did) the cause must be God. Now a great deal of ink has been spilt on this problem, with wise men saying that there is in the unconscious a cause that we cannot detect. This is an interesting psychological problem, but here I only want to draw your attention to the practical issue. There seemed to be no cause for Paul's enlightenment on the road to Damascus. There seemed to be no cause for the disciples leaving their nets to follow Jesus. And so in your life and the lives of those you direct, you may find yourself saying things without knowing why you say them, or doing things without knowing why you do them. Or you may make a decision without knowing why you made it. Yet you have the unshakeable conviction that what you said or did was right, or that your decision was authentic. These are completely spontaneous actions done under the guidance of the Spirit. And this is consolation without previous cause. It is a mystical gift.

In the Gospel Jesus encourages us to expect this kind of gift. He tells us that when we are brought before princes and kings (or when we are in a fix) we should not reason and think about what we are going to say, for in that hour the Holy Spirit will tell us. So don't be anxious and full of rationalization. Wait for the Spirit. God is faithful: he will not let you down.

Ignatius says nothing about discernment of dreams, but this can be important for contemporary people. If you have an important dream, it is good to write it down and bring it before your mind's eye in meditation. Ask the Holy Spirit for light to discern; and you may then discover that your unconscious is very wisely pointing the direction in which you must go.

* * *

In these pages I have spoken about individual discernment wherein you make a decision to choose a path in life. However, in the New Testament discernment is not only individual but also communal: the community discerns and decides. This is particularly evident in The Acts of the Apostles where we read that the group, moved by the Spirit, sent out Paul and Barnabas. How conscious they were of the inner movements within the community as a whole! And then there were prophets like Agabus to whom they listened with attention. Later when Paul was travelling with his disciples and friends, the whole group felt instinctively that the Spirit of Jesus did not want them to preach the word in Bithynia or in Asia Minor, or they felt that the Spirit did call them to Macedonia. Here was a community in touch with the Spirit and constantly discerning His guidance and His voice.

And in the modern world the practice of communal discernment is again coming to the fore. Needless to say, it presupposes a group of people who love one another, pray together and are attentive to the action of the Spirit in the community. It presupposes a group of people who are sensitive to the charismatic gifts of its members. I cannot give you concrete advice about this process, Thomas; but I urge you to give it prayerful thought and consideration. For communal discernment is the way of the future.

TWENTY

---------- ✳ ----------

Social Consciousness

Modern people are very conscious of the social problems of our day. We are acutely aware of the shocking problems of hunger, unemployment, nuclear war, the arms race, terrorism, political oppression, torture. We are aware of the inhumanity and barbarism that have characterized our century; and we realize that, thanks to our greed and stupidity, the very survival of the human race is at stake.

There are always some good people who shake sad and cynical heads with the comment: "And while the world is in such a mess you sit in wordless silence. Yes, you enter your cloud of unknowing and bury everything beneath your little cloud of forgetting! You extol being above doing. You glorify imageless prayer and abandon discursive thinking. And you enter your dark night. How can you do such a thing? How can you be indifferent to the plight of millions of your brothers and sisters on this earth – millions of your brothers and sisters who are also God's children?"

And in the pages of this book I have attempted to give some answer to these questions. I have said that silent and imageless meditation leads to a profound conversion like that of the Good Samaritan who picked up the poor traveller lying bleeding by the roadside. It opens our hearts to compassion for every single human being who suffers in the whole world. Through authentic compassion you suffer with (and the word "compassion" means just that); and you are never far from the one who is in agony and pain.

Again, I have said that being is constructive and creative, just as suffering is creative and brings forth its child.

Again, I have said that prayer leads to enlightenment and wisdom. And who could deny that what our poor world needs is men and women of wisdom? That is to say, we need men and women who will see the problem at its roots without undue influence from the fluctuating and fickle world of public opinion.

Again, I have pointed to the great symbolic event of Assisi where representatives of all the great religions manifested their belief in the power of prayer. They proclaimed to humankind that more is wrought by prayer than this world dreams on.

Again, I have said that prayer will liberate you from the discouragement, the sadness, the depression that so often settle on people who undertake great tasks for the world and for God. It will liberate you from the consuming anger that leads to violence and destruction. Prayer will give you joy in difficult enterprises and peace in the midst of failure.

Having said all this, however, I must also say that some problems remain. Criticism of silent prayer is not always without foundation. For the fact, the obvious fact, is that wordless, mystical contemplation, however deep, will not put you in touch with the actualities and concrete problems of our day. It needs to be complemented by study, by observation of the world, by attentiveness to the signs of the times, by reading, by what I have called essential prayer. In short, existential prayer does not stand alone. And if we think it does, we shall be in trouble.

This points to something of the greatest importance for those who enter the mystical path. So let me put it schematically. There is –

A way of silence and a way of words

A way of darkness and a way of light

A way of negation and a way of affirmation

A way of unknowing and a way of knowing

A way of mysticism and a way of theology

A way of no object and a way of object

A way of being and a way of doing

A way of existence and a way of essence

A way of timelessness and a way of time

An apophatic way and a kataphatic way

And so it goes on.

In these pages, wherein I have dealt mainly with mysticism, the stress has fallen on silence, darkness, negation, unknowing and the rest. But the point I want to make now is that silence and darkness, negation and unknowing need to be complemented by words and light, affirmation and knowing. If you concentrate on one to the exclusion of the other you become horribly one-sided. Biologists might say that you are using one side of your brain to the exclusion of the other. Let me again put it schematically:

Silence needs words

Darkness needs light

Negation needs affirmation

Unknowing needs knowing

Intuition needs reason

Mysticism needs theology

Timelessness needs time

Non-objective prayer needs objective prayer

Existence needs essence

The feminine needs the masculine

Yin needs Yang

No one can spend his or her whole life in a cloud of forgetting. Human consciousness is, indeed, in constant flux. It floats from silence to words, from darkness to light, from negation to affirmation.

And now let me come to practicalities. I have urged you to enter into silent, existential prayer when you are called to do so. I have said that prayer in a cloud of unknowing is precious beyond words. All this I reaffirm. But now I want to add that, if you want to be an authentic human being, you must study in order to develop the essential dimension of your personality.

On this point, however, let me warn you against pious mystics who will tell you that study is an obstacle to contemplation and that you would spend your time to greater advantage by abandoning all reading in order to chop wood, carry water and dig potatoes. And their contention may be all the more beguiling when you find in yourself a great reluctance to study, just as you have a great reluctance to engage in discursive prayer. But look on this, Thomas, as a temptation and a snare. Devote some time to study each day even if you must force yourself to do so, even if you are longing to sit on your cushion in silent contemplation and the absence of thought.

I advise you first to study the modern world. Become aware of the cruel sufferings of millions of oppressed people. If you get the opportunity, go to Manila or Calcutta and witness poverty with your own two eyes. Familiarize yourself with the work of organizations like Amnesty International. Develop a sense for injustice wherever it is, but particularly in your own household.

And in the context of the modern suffering world, read the scriptures. Read them again and again, and you will find that they lead you to enlightenment – not to an enlightenment like that of Saint John of the Cross or even Saint Paul, but to an enlightenment that is vitally valid in our day. Take, for example, the text "Blessed are the peacemakers . . ." (Matthew 5:9). What new splendour this takes on in our modern times! If you meditate on the text while keeping in touch with the modern scene you may come to the radical conversion of a Mahatma Gandhi or a Martin Luther King.

But sacred scripture is not the only enlightened text. I urge you also to read and re-read the papers of the Second Vatican Council, particularly *The Church in the Modern World*. Here you will find the gospel message expressed in a modern context. Let the words and symbols sink into your unconscious so that they will live within when you sit in silent meditation. By this and other enlightened texts you will find you are transformed and converted. You will find that you are filled with compassion, not for humanity in the abstract but for the men and women and children who are suffering throughout today's world.

I have spoken at some length about discernment; and now let me add that discernment is of capital importance here. When you view the enormous social problems that confront us today you will immediately realize that little you or little me cannot take responsibility for the sufferings of the whole world. We must select; and we must select according to the guidance of the Spirit. As you know, there are broadly two approaches to our suffering world. There is the approach of people like Mother Teresa of Calcutta or Bob Geldof of Dublin, who try concretely to help the starving millions or the sick or the dying. And there is the other more delicate approach of those who attempt to change the wicked structures of modern society or to raise the consciousness of the oppressed. In both of these approaches you will need God's grace; for you will meet with opposition and criticism and even threats that would crush the most courageous. But if you listen carefully to what I have said about discernment you will find your own unique and special way. You may even find that you have a message for the modern world which is *your* message and which you must proclaim, even if you suffer and die.

Let me conclude with two observations.

The first is that all the social problems in the world are finally rooted in evil. And some kinds of evil are only driven out by prayer and fasting.

The second is that it is more important to change hearts than to change systems. But we cannot change hearts, even our own. Only God can change hearts. And He does so in answer to prayer.

INDEX

BOOKS BY WILLIAM JOHNSTON

Silent Music

A brilliant synthesis which joins traditional religious insights with the discoveries of modern science to provide a complete picture of mysticism – its techniques and stages, its mental and physical aspects, its dangers, and its consequences.

The Inner Eye of Love

"This is a lucid comparison and exposition of eastern and western mysticism, from Zen to the Cloud of Unknowing, which can do nothing but good all round."

Gerald Priestland, The Universe

The Mirror Mind

"William Johnston continues his first-hand studies of Zen meditation and Christian prayer . . . At his disposal he has had a twofold large and demanding literature. His use of it can be startlingly luminous."

Bernard Lonegan

The Wounded Stag

This book examines the Old and New Testaments, the Christian mystical tradition, the Eucharist and mystical prayer, and explains how these can lead to the resolution of the conflict within men's hearts. A book with a message for today.

I Believe
Trevor Huddleston

A simple, prayerful series of reflections on the phrases of the Creed. This is a beautiful testament of the strong, quiet inner faith of a man best known for his active role in the Church – and in the world.

The Heart of the Christian Faith
Donald Coggan

The author ". . . presents the essential core of Christianity in a marvellously simple and readable form, quite uncluttered by any excess of theological technicality."

The Yorkshire Post

Be Still and Know
Michael Ramsey

The former Archbishop of Canterbury looks at prayer in the New Testament, at what the early mystics could teach us about it, and at some practical aspects of Christian praying.

Pilgrim's Progress
John Bunyan

"A masterpiece which generation after generation of ordinary men and women have taken to their hearts."

Hugh Ross Williamson

Also available in Fount Paperbacks

The Sacrament of the Present Moment
JEAN-PIERRE DE CAUSSADE

'It is good to have this classic from the days of the Quietist tensions with its thesis that we can and must find God in the totality of our immediate situation . . .'

The Expository Times

The Poems of St John of the Cross
TRANSLATED BY ROY CAMPBELL

'Mr Campbell has recreated the extraordinary subtlety of the music of the original in an English verse worthy of it and that climbs from aspiration to ecstasy as if it were itself the poem.'

The Guardian

Thérèse of Lisieux
MICHAEL HOLLINGS

A superb portrait of one of the most popular of all saints.

'This book is well worth recommending . . . presents a simple factual outline of Thérèse's life and teaching . . . (with) incidents . . . applied to our own everyday lives.'

Review for Contemplatives of all Traditions

I, Francis
CARLO CARRETTO

This unusual and compelling book is a sustained meditation on the spirituality of St Francis of Assisi, bringing the meaning of his message to our time.

'A book one will not forget.'

Eric Doyle, The Tablet